# Differentiating Instruction With Menus

# Language Arts

# Differentiating Instruction With Menus

# Language Arts

Laurie E. Westphal

PRUFROCK PRESS INC.
WACO, TEXAS

Library of Congress Cataloging-in-Publication Data

Westphal, Laurie E., 1967–
    Differentiating instruction with menus. Language arts / Laurie E. Westphal.
        p. cm.
    Includes bibliographical references.
    ISBN-13: 978-1-59363-225-0 (pbk.)
    ISBN-10: 1-59363-225-8 (pbk.)
    1.  English language—Composition and exercises—Study and teaching. 2.  Language arts—
Correlation with content subjects. 3.  Individualized instruction. 4.  Curriculum planning.
I. Title.
    LB1576.W4845 2007
    372.6--dc22

                        2007016523

Edited by Jennifer Robins
Production Design by Marjorie Parker

ISBN-13: 978-1-59363-225-0
ISBN-10: 1-59363-225-8

At the time of this book's publication, all facts and figures cited are the most current available; all telephone numbers, addresses, and Web site URLs are accurate and active; all publications, organizations, Web sites, and other resources exist as described in this book; and all have been verified. The authors and Prufrock Press make no warranty or guarantee concerning the information and materials given out by organizations or content found at Web sites, and we are not responsible for any changes that occur after this book's publication. If you find an error or believe that a resource listed here is not as described, please contact Prufrock Press.

Prufrock Press Inc.
P.O. Box 8813
Waco, TX 76714-8813
Phone: (800) 998-2208
Fax: (800) 240-0333
http://www.prufrock.com

# CONTENTS

# CHAPTER 1

# Choice

"**O**h my gosh! THAAAAANK YOU!" exclaimed one of my students as he fell to his knees dramatically in the middle of my classroom. I had just had handed out a list menu on the periodic table and told my students they would be able to choose how they wanted to learn the material.

## Why Is Choice Important?

Ask adults whether they would prefer to choose what to do or be told what to do, and of course, they are going to say they would prefer to have a choice. Students have the same feelings. Although they may not stand up and demand a choice if none is present, they benefit in many ways from having them.

One benefit of choice is its ability to meet the needs of so many different students and their learning styles. The Dunedin College of Education (Keen, 2001) conducted a research study on the preferred learning styles of 250 gifted students. Students were asked to rank different learning options. Of the 13 different options described to the students, only one option did not receive at least one negative response, and that was the option of having choice. Although all students have different learning styles and preferences, choice is the one option that meets all students' needs. Students are going to choose what best fits their learning styles and educational needs.

> " . . . I am different in the way I do stuff. I like to build stuff with my hands. . . ."
>
> —*Sixth-grade student, when asked why he enjoyed activities that allow choice.*

Another benefit of choice is a greater sense of independence for the students. What a powerful feeling! Students will be designing and creating a product based on what they envision, rather than what their teacher envisions. When students would enter my middle-school classroom, they often had been trained by previous teachers to produce exactly what the teacher wanted, not what the students thought would be best. Teaching my students that what they envision could be correct (and wonderful) was often a struggle. "Is this what you want?" or "Is this right?" were popular questions as we started the school year. Allowing students to have choices in the products they create to show their learning helps create independence at an early age.

Strengthened student focus on the required content is a third benefit. When students have choices in the activities they wish to complete, they are more focused on the learning that leads to their choice product. Students become excited when they learn information that can help them develop a product they would like to create. Students pay close attention to instruction and have an immediate application for the knowledge being presented in class. Also, if students are focused, they are less likely to be off task during instruction.

Many a great educator has referred to the idea that the best learning takes place when the students have a desire to learn. Some students have a desire to learn anything that is new to them; others do not want to learn anything unless it is of interest to them. By incorporating different activities from which to choose, students stretch beyond what they already know, and teachers create a void that needs to be filled. This void leads to a desire to learn.

## How Can Teachers Provide Choices?

> "The GT students seem to get more involved in assignments when they have choice. They have so many creative ideas and the menus give them the opportunity to use them."
>
> —Social studies teacher, when asked how students respond to having choices.

When people go to a restaurant, the common goal is to find something on the menu to satisfy their hunger. Students come into our classrooms having a hunger, as well—a hunger for learning. Choice menus are a way of allowing our students to choose how they would like to satisfy that hunger. At the very least, a menu is a list of choices that students use to choose an activity (or activities) they would like to complete to show what they have learned. At best, it is a complex system in which students earn points by making choices from different areas of study. All menus should also incorporate a free-choice option for those "picky eaters" who would like to make a special order to satisfy their learning hunger.

The next few sections provide examples of the main types of menus that will be used in this book. Each menu has its own benefits, limitations or drawbacks, and time considerations. An explanation of the free-choice option and its management will follow the information on each type of menu.

## Tic-Tac-Toe Menu

> "Sometimes I only liked two, but I had to do three."
>
> —Second-grade student, when asked what he liked least about a menu used in his classroom.

### Description

The Tic-Tac-Toe Menu (see Figure 1.1) is a basic menu that contains a total of eight predetermined choices and one free choice for students.

All choices are created at the same level of Bloom's Revised taxonomy (Anderson et al., 2001). Each choice carries the same weight for grading and has similar expectations for completion time and effort.

## Benefits

*Flexibility.* This menu can cover one topic in depth or three different objectives. When this menu covers just one objective, students have the option of completing three projects in a tic-tac-toe pattern, or simply picking three from the menu. When it covers three objectives, students will need to complete a tic-tac-toe pattern (one in each column or row) to be sure they have completed one activity from each objective.

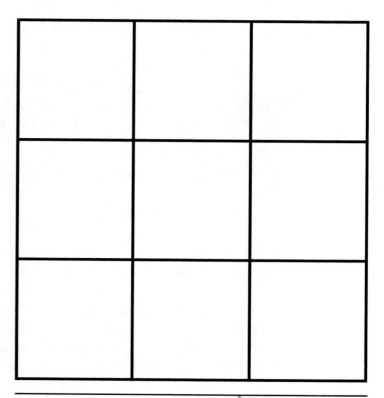

Figure 1.1. Tic-tac-toe menu

*Friendly Design.* Students quickly understand how to use this menu.

*Weighting.* All projects are equally weighted, so recording grades and maintaining paperwork is easily accomplished with this menu.

## Limitations

*Few Topics.* These menus only cover one or three topics.

*Short Time Period.* They are intended for shorter periods of time, between 1–3 weeks.

*Student Compromise.* Although this menu does allow choice, a student will sometimes have to compromise and complete an activity he or she would not have chosen because it completes the required tic-tac-toe. (This is not always bad, though!)

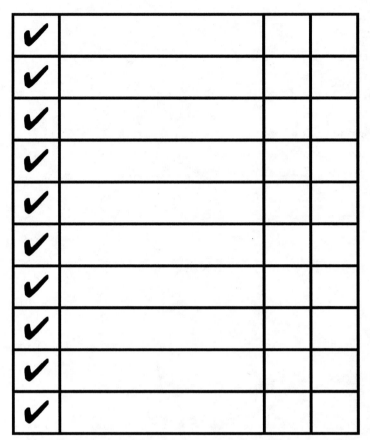

Figure 1.2. List menu

*Time Considerations*

These menus are usually intended for shorter amounts of completion time—at the most, they should take 3 weeks. If it focuses on one topic in depth, the menu can be completed in one week.

## List Menu

*Description*

The List Menu (see Figure 1.2), or Challenge List, is a more complex menu than the Tic-Tac-Toe Menu, with a total of at least 10 predetermined choices, each with its own point value, and at least one free choice for students. Choices are simply listed with assigned points based on the levels of Bloom's Revised taxonomy. The choices carry different weights and have different expectations for completion time and effort. A point criterion is set forth that equals 100%, and students choose how they wish to attain that point goal.

*Benefits*

*Responsibility.* Students have complete control over their grades. They really like the idea that they can guarantee their grade if they complete the required work. If they lose points on one of the chosen assignments, they can complete another to be sure they have met their goal points.

*Concept Reinforcement.* This menu also allows for an in-depth study of material; however, with the different levels of Bloom's Revised taxonomy being represented, students who are still learning the concepts can choose some of the lower level point value projects to reinforce the basics before jumping into the higher level activities.

### Limitations

*Few Topics.* This menu is best used for one topic in depth, although it can be used for up to three different topics, as well.

*Cannot Guarantee Objectives.* If it is used for three topics, it is possible for a student to not have to complete an activity for each objective, depending on the choices he or she makes.

*Preparation.* Teachers need to have all materials ready at the beginning of the unit for students to be able to choose any of the activities on the list, which requires advance planning.

### Time Considerations

The List Menus are usually intended for shorter amounts of completion time—at the most, 2 weeks.

## 2-5-8 Menu

> "My favorite menu is the 2-5-8 kind. It's easy to understand and I can pick just what I want to do."
>
> —*Fourth-grade student, when asked about his favorite type of menu.*

### Description

A 2-5-8 Menu (see Figure 1.3) is a variation of the List Menu, with a total of at least eight predetermined choices: at least two choices with a point value of two, at least four choices with a point value of five, and at least two choices with a point value of eight. Choices are assigned points based on the levels of Bloom's Revised taxonomy (Anderson et al., 2001). Choices with a point value of two represent the *remember* and *understand* levels, choices with a point value of five represent the *apply* and *analyze* levels, and choices with a point value of eight represent the *evaluate* and *create* levels. All levels of choices carry different weights and have different expectations for completion time and effort. Students are expected to earn 10 points for a 100%.

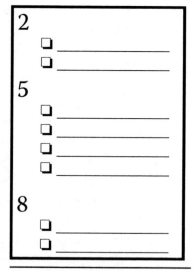

Figure 1.3. 2-5-8 menu

Students choose what combination they would like to use to attain that point goal.

### Benefits

*Responsibility.* With this menu, students still have complete control over their grades.

*Guaranteed Activity.* This menu's design is also set up in such a way that students must complete at least one activity at a higher level of Bloom's Revised taxonomy in order to reach their point goal.

### Limitations

*One Topic.* Although it can be used for more than one topic, this menu works best with in-depth study of one topic.

*No Free Choice.* By nature, it does not allow students to propose their own free choice, because point values need to be assigned based on Bloom's Revised taxonomy.

*Higher Level Thinking.* Students will complete only one activity at a higher level of thinking.

### Time Considerations

The 2-5-8 Menus are usually intended for a shorter amount of completion time—at the most, one week.

## Game Show Menu

"This menu really challenged my students. If one of my students saw another student choosing a more difficult option, they wanted to choose one, too. I had very few students choose the basic options on this menu. It was wonderful!"

*—Sixth-grade science teacher*

## Description

The Game Show Menu (see Figure 1.4) is the most complex menu. It covers multiple topics or objectives with at least three predetermined choices and a free student choice for each objective. Choices are assigned points based on the levels of Bloom's taxonomy. All choices carry different weights and have different expectations for completion time and effort. A point criterion is set forth that equals 100%. Students must complete at least one activity from each objective in order to reach their goal.

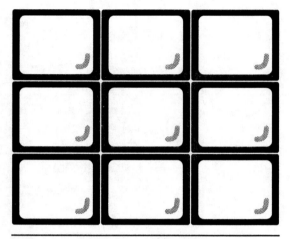

Figure 1.4. Game show menu

## Benefits

*Free Choice.* This menu allows many choices for students, but if they do not want to complete the offered activities, they can propose their own activity for each objective.

*Responsibility.* This menu also allows students to guarantee their own grades.

*Different Learning Levels.* It also has the flexibility to allow for individualized contracts for different learning levels within the classroom. Each student can contract for a certain number of points for his or her grade.

*Objectives Guaranteed.* The teacher is also guaranteed that the students complete an activity from each objective covered, even if it is at a lower level.

## Limitations

*Confirm Expectations.* The only real limitation here is that students (and parents) must understand the guidelines for completing the menu.

## Time Considerations

These menus are usually intended for a longer amount of completion time. Although they can be used as a yearlong menu (each column could be a grading period), they are usually intended for 4–6 weeks.

## Free Choice

> *" . . . the free choice. I love it, love it!!! I got to do what I really wanted to! [The teacher] let me reserch [sic] my own book."*
>
> *—Second-grade student, when asked what she liked most about the menu students had just completed.*

With most of the menus, the students are allowed to submit a free choice for their teacher's consideration. Figure 1.5 shows two sample proposal forms that have been used many times successfully in my classroom. The form used is based on the type of menu being presented. If students are using the Tic-Tac-Toe Menu, there is no need to submit a point proposal. A copy of these forms should be given to each student when each menu is first introduced. A discussion should be held with the students so they understand the expectations of a free choice. If students do not want to make a proposal using the proposal form after the teacher has discussed the entire menu and its activities, they can place the unused form in a designated place in the classroom. Others may want to use their form, and it is often surprising who wants to submit a proposal form after hearing about the opportunity!

Proposal forms must be submitted before students begin working on their free-choice products. The teacher then knows what the students are working on and the student knows the expectations the teacher has for that product. Once approved, the forms can easily be stapled to the student's menu sheet. The students can refer to it as they develop their free-choice product, and when the grading takes place, the teacher can refer to the agreement for the "graded" features of the product.

Each part of the proposal form is important and needs to be discussed with students:

- *Name/Teacher's Approval.* The student must submit this form to the teacher for approval. The teacher will carefully review all of the information, send it back to the student for correction, if needed, and then sign the top.
- *Points Requested.* Found only on the point-based menu proposal form, this is usually where negotiation needs to take place. Students usually will submit their first request for a very high number (even the 100% goal.) They really do equate the amount of time something

Name _____     Teacher's Approval: _____

## Free-Choice Proposal Form for Point-Based Menu

Points Requested: _____     Points Approved: _____

Proposal Outline

1. What specific topic or idea will you learn about?

2. What criteria should be used to grade it? (Neatness, content, creativity, artistic value, etc.)

3. What will your product look like?

4. What materials will you need from the teacher to create this product?

Name _____     Teacher's Approval: _____

## Free-Choice Proposal Form

Proposal Outline

1. What specific topic or idea will you learn about?

2. What criteria should be used to grade it? (Neatness, content, creativity, artistic value, etc.)

3. What will your product look like?

4. What materials will you need from the teacher to create this product?

Figure 1.5. Sample proposal forms

will take with the amount of points it should earn. But, please note, the points are *always* based on the levels of Bloom's Revised taxonomy. For example, a PowerPoint presentation with a vocabulary word quiz would get minimal points, although it may have taken a long time to create. If the students have not been exposed to the levels of Bloom's Revised taxonomy, this can be difficult to explain. You can always refer to the popular "Bloom's Verbs" to help explain the difference between time requirements and higher level activities.

- *Points Approved.* Found only on the point-based menu proposal form, this is the final decision recorded by the teacher once the point haggling is finished.
- *Proposal Outline.* This is where the student will tell you everything about the product he or she intends to complete. These questions should be completed in such a way that you can really picture what the student is planning on completing. This also shows you that the student knows what he or she is planning on completing.
  - *What specific topic or idea will you learn about?* Students need to be specific here. It is not acceptable to write *science* or *reading*. This is where they look at the objectives of the project and chose which objective their project demonstrates.
  - *What criteria should be used to grade it?* Although there are rubrics for all of the projects that the students might create, it is important for the students to explain what criteria are most important to evaluate the product. The student may indicate that the rubric being used for all the predetermined projects is fine; however, he or she may also want to add other criteria here.
  - *What will your product look like?* It is important that this be as detailed as possible. If a student cannot express what it will "look like," he or she has probably not given the free-choice plan enough thought.
  - *What materials will you need from the teacher to create this product?* This is an important consideration. Sometimes students do not have the means to purchase items for their project. This can be negotiated, as well, but if you ask what students may need, they often will develop even grander ideas for their free choice.

## 3 Ways to Use Menus

1.) Enrichment and Supplementary activities

2.) Menus can be used to replace certain curricular activities used to teach content

3.) Menus can be used as mini-lessons to accompany classroom activities

# CHAPTER 2

# How to Use Menus in the Classroom

There are different ways to use instructional menus in the classroom. In order to decide how to implement each menu, the following questions should be considered: How much prior knowledge of the topic being taught do the students have before the unit or lesson begins and how much information is readily available for students to obtain on their own?

There are three customary ways to use menus in the classroom. Using them for enrichment and supplementary activities is the most common. In this case, the students usually do not have a lot of background knowledge and the information about the topic may not be readily available to all students. The teacher will introduce the menu and the activities at the beginning of a unit. The teacher will then progress through the content at the normal rate, using his or her own curricular materials and periodically allowing class time and homework time throughout the unit for students to work on their menu choices to supplement a deeper understanding of the lessons being taught. This method is very effective, as it builds in an immediate use for the content the teacher is covering. For example, at the beginning of a unit on the Civil War, the teacher many introduce the menu with the explanation that students may not have all of the knowledge to complete all of their choices yet. During the unit, however, more content will be provided and they will be prepared to work on new choices. If students want to work ahead, they certainly can find the information on their own, but that is not required. Gifted students often see this as a challenge and will begin to investigate concepts mentioned in the menu before the teacher discusses them. This helps build an immense pool of background knowledge before the topic is even discussed in the classroom. As teachers, we fight the battle of having students read ahead or "come to class prepared to discuss." By introducing a menu at the beginning of a unit and allowing students to complete products as instruction progresses, the students naturally investigate the information and come to class prepared without it being a completely separate requirement.

Another option for using menus in the classroom is to replace certain curricular activities the teacher uses to teach the specified content. In this case, the students may have some limited background knowledge about the content and information is readily available for them in their classroom resources. The teacher would pick and choose which aspects of the content must be directly taught to the students, and which could be appropriately learned and reinforced through product menus. The unit is then designed using both formal instructional lessons and specific menu days where the students will use the menu to reinforce the prior knowledge they already have learned. In order for this option to be effective, the teacher must feel very comfortable with the students' prior knowledge level. Another variation on this method is using the menus to drive center or station activities. Centers have many different functions in the classroom—most importantly reinforcing the instruction that has taken place. Rather than having a set rotation for centers, the teacher could use the menu activities as enrichment or supplementary activities during center time for those students who need more than just reinforcement; centers could be set up with the materials students would need to complete various products.

The third option for menu use is the use of mini-lessons, with the menus driving the accompanying classroom activities. This method is best used when the majority of the students have a lot of prior knowledge about the topic. The teacher can design 10–15 minute mini-lessons, where students quickly review basic concepts that are already familiar to them. The students are then turned loose to choose an activity on the menu to show they understand the concept. The game show menu usually works very well with this method of instruction, as the topics across the top usually lend themselves to the mini-lessons. It is important that the students have prior knowledge on the content because the lesson cycle is cut very short in this use of menus. Using menus in this way does not allow teachers to use the guided practice step of the lesson, as it is assumed the students already understand the information. The teacher is simply reviewing the information and then moving right to the higher levels of Bloom's Revised taxonomy by asking students to create a product. By using the menus in this way, the teacher avoids the "I already know this" glossy looks from his or her students. Another important consideration is the independence level of the students. In order for this use of menus to be effective, students will need to be able to work independently for up to 30 minutes after the mini-lesson. Because students are often interested in the product they have chosen, this is not a critical issue, but still one worth mentioning as teachers consider how they would like to use various menus in their classroom.

# CHAPTER 3

# Guidelines for Products

"... each project is unique."

*—Fifth-grade student, when asked why he enjoys choice menus.*

This chapter outlines the different types of products included in the featured menus, as well as the guidelines and expectations for each. It is very important that students know exactly what the expectations of a completed product are when they choose to work on it. By discussing these expectations *before* students begin and having the information readily available ahead of time, you will limit the frustration on everyone's part.

## $1 Contract

Consideration should be given to the cost of creating the products featured on any menu. The resources available to students vary within a classroom, and students should not be graded on the amount of materials they can purchase to make a product look better. These menus are designed to equalize the resources students have available. The materi-

---

### $1 Contract

I did not spend more than $1.00 on my _____.

_____     _____
            Student Signature                              Date

My child, _____, did not spend more than $1.00 on the product he or she created.

_____     _____
            Parent Signature                               Date

**Figure 3.1. $1 contract**

als for most products are available for less than a dollar and can often be found in a teacher's classroom as part of the classroom supplies. If a product requires materials from the student, there is a $1 contract as part of the product criteria. This is a very important piece in the explanation of the product. First of all, by limiting the amount of money a child can spend, it creates an equal amount of resources for all students. Second, it actually encourages a more creative product. When students are limited by the amount of materials they can readily purchase, they often have to use materials from home in new and unique ways. Figure 3.1 is a sample of the contract that has been used many times in my classroom with various products.

## The Products

Table 3.1 contains a list of the products used in this book. These products were chosen for their flexibility in meeting learning styles, as well as for being products many teachers are already using in their classroom. They have been arranged by learning style—visual, kinesthetic, or auditory—and each menu has been designed to include products from all of the learning styles. Of course, some of the products may be listed in more than one area depending on how they are presented or implemented. The specific expectations for all of the products are presented in an easy-to-

**Table 3.1**
# Products

| Visual | Kinesthetic | Auditory |
|---|---|---|
| Acrostic | Commercial | Commercial |
| Advertisement | Concentration Cards | Interview |
| Book Cover | Diorama | News Report |
| Brochure/Pamphlet | Flipbook | Play |
| Cartoon/Comic Strip | Game | PowerPoint— Presentation |
| Collage | Mobile | |
| Crossword Puzzle | Model | Puppet |
| Greeting Card | Play | Song/Rap |
| Letter | Product Cube | Speech |
| Map | Puppet | You Be the Person Presentation |
| Mind Map | Student-Taught Lesson | |
| Newspaper Article | Three-Dimensional Timeline | Video |
| Poster | Video | |
| PowerPoint— Stand Alone | | |
| Questionnaire | | |
| Recipe/Recipe Card | | |
| Scrapbook | | |
| Story | | |
| Trading Cards | | |
| Venn Diagram | | |
| Video | | |
| Window Pane | | |
| Worksheet | | |

read card format that can be reproduced for students (see Figure 3.2). This format is convenient for students to have in front of them when they work on their projects. These cards also can be laminated and posted on a bulletin board for easy access during classroom work.

| Acrostic | Advertisement | Book Cover |
|---|---|---|
| • At least 8.5" x 11"<br>• Neatly written or typed<br>• Target word will be written down the left side of the paper<br>• Each descriptive word chosen must begin with one of the letters from the target word<br>• Each descriptive word chosen must be related to the target word | • At least 8.5" x 11"<br>• A slogan should be included<br>• Color picture of item or service should be included<br>• Include price, if appropriate<br>• Can be developed on the computer | • Front Cover—title, author, and image<br>• Cover Inside Flap—summary of the book<br>• Back Inside Flap—brief biography of the author<br>• Back Cover—editorial comments about the book<br>• Spine—title and author |
| **Brochure/Pamphlet** | **Cartoon/Comic Strip** | **Collage** |
| • At least 8.5" x 11"<br>• Must be in three-fold format; front fold has the title and picture<br>• Must have both pictures and written text<br>• Information should be in paragraph form with at least five facts included | • At least 8.5" x 11"<br>• Should have at least six cells<br>• Must have meaningful dialogue<br>• Must include color | • At least 8.5" x 11"<br>• Pictures must be neatly cut from magazines or newspapers (no clip art)<br>• Label items as required in task |
| **Commercial** | **Concentration Cards** | **Crossword Puzzle** |
| • Must be 5–10 minutes in length<br>• Script must be turned in before commercial is presented<br>• Can be presented live to an audience or recorded<br>• Props or some form of costume must be used<br>• Can include more than one person | • At least 20 index cards (10 matching sets) must be made<br>• Both pictures and words can be used<br>• Information should be placed on just one side of each card<br>• Include an answer key that shows the matches<br>• All cards must be submitted in a carrying bag | • At least 20 significant words or phrases should be included<br>• Develop appropriate clues<br>• Include puzzle and answer key |
| **Diorama** | **Flipbook** | **Game** |
| • At least 4" x 5" x 8"<br>• Must be self-standing<br>• All interior space must be covered with relevant pictures and information<br>• Name written on the back in permanent ink<br>• Informational/title card attached to diorama | • At least 8.5" x 11" folded in half<br>• All information or opinions are supported by facts<br>• Created with the correct number of flaps cut into the top<br>• Color is optional<br>• Name must be written on the back | • At least four thematic game pieces<br>• At least 25 colored/thematic squares<br>• At least 20 question/activity cards<br>• Include a thematic title on the board<br>• Include a complete set of rules for playing the game<br>• At least the size of an open file folder (11" x 17") |

Figure 3.2. Product guidelines

| Greeting Card | Interview | Letter |
|---|---|---|
| • Front—colored pictures, words optional<br>• Front Inside—personal note related to topic<br>• Back Inside—greeting or saying; must meet product criteria<br>• Back Outside—logo, publisher, and price for card | • Must have at least five questions relevant to the topic begin studied<br>• Questions and answers must be neatly written or typed | • Neatly written or typed<br>• Uses proper letter format<br>• At least three paragraphs in length<br>• Must follow type of letter stated in the menu (e.g., friendly, persuasive, informational) |
| **Map** | **Mind Map** | **Mobile** |
| • At least 8.5" x 11"<br>• Accurate information is included<br>• Includes at least 10 relevant locations<br>• Includes compass rose, legend, scale, and key | • At least 8.5" x 11"<br>• Must have one central idea<br>• Follow the "no more than four" rule—no more than four words coming from any one word | • At least 10 pieces of related information<br>• Includes color and pictures<br>• Has at least three layers of hanging information<br>• Hangs in a balanced way |
| **Model** | **News Report** | **Newspaper Article** |
| • At least 8" x 8" x 12"<br>• Parts of model must be labeled, and should be in scale when appropriate<br>• Must include a title card<br>• Name written on model in ink | • Must address the who, what, where, when, why, and how of the topic<br>• Script of report turned in with project, or before, if performance will be "live"<br>• Must be either performed live or recorded | • Must be informational in nature<br>• Must follow standard newspaper format<br>• Must include picture with caption that supports article<br>• At least three paragraphs in length<br>• Neatly written or typed |
| **Play** | **Poster** | **PowerPoint—Stand Alone** |
| • Must be between 5–10 minutes long<br>• Script must be turned in before play is presented<br>• Must be presented to an audience<br>• Should have props or some form of costume<br>• Can include more than one person | • Should be the size of a standard poster board<br>• Includes at least five pieces of important information<br>• Must have title<br>• Must contain both words and pictures<br>• Name must be written on the back | • At least 10 informational slides and one title slide with student's name<br>• No more than 15 words per page<br>• Slides must have color and at least one graphic per page<br>• Animation is optional, and should not distract from information being presented |

Figure 3.2. Product guidelines

| PowerPoint—Presentation | Product Cube | Puppet |
|---|---|---|
| • At least 10 informational slides and one title slide with student's name<br>• No more than 15 words per page<br>• Slides must have color and at least one graphic per page<br>• Animation is optional, and should not distract from information being presented<br>• Presentation should be timed and flow with the oral presentation | • All six sides of the cube must be filled with information<br>• Name must be printed neatly at the bottom of one of the sides of the cube | • Puppet should be handmade and must have a moveable mouth<br>• A list of supplies used to make the puppet must be turned in with the puppet<br>• If used in a play, all play criteria must be met, as well. |
| **Questionnaire** | **Recipe/Recipe Card** | **Scrapbook** |
| • Neatly written or typed<br>• Includes at least 10 questions with possible answers, and at least one question that requires a written response<br>• Questions must be helpful to gathering information on the topic being studied | • Must be written neatly or typed on a piece of paper or an index card<br>• Must have a list of ingredients with measurements for each<br>• Must have numbered steps that explain how to make the recipe | • Cover of scrapbook must have a meaningful title and the student's name<br>• Must have at least five themed pages<br>• Each page will have at least one picture<br>• All photos will have captions |
| **Song/Rap** | **Speech** | **Story** |
| • Words must make sense<br>• Can be presented to an audience or taped<br>• Written words will be turned in before performance or with taped song<br>• Should be at least 2 minutes in length | • Must be at least 2 minutes in length<br>• Should not be read from written paper<br>• Note cards can be used<br>• Written speech must be turned in before speech is presented<br>• Voice must be clear, loud, and easy to understand | • Must be neatly written or typed<br>• Must have all of the elements of a well-written story (setting, characters, problem, events, and solution)<br>• Must be appropriate length to allow for story elements |
| **Three-Dimensional Timeline** | **Trading Cards** | **Venn Diagram** |
| • Must be no bigger than a standard-size poster board<br>• Should be divided into equal time units<br>• Must contain at least 10 important dates and have at least two sentences explaining why each date is important<br>• Must have an meaningful, creative object securely attached beside each date to represent that date<br>• Must be able to explain how each object represents each date | • Includes at least 10 cards<br>• Each card should be at least 3" x 5"<br>• Each should have a colored picture<br>• Includes at least three facts on the subject of the card<br>• Cards must have information on both sides<br>• All cards must be submitted in a carrying bag | • At least 8.5" x 11"<br>• Shapes should be thematic and neatly drawn<br>• Must have a title for the entire diagram and a title for each section<br>• Must have at least six items in each section of the diagram<br>• Name must be written on the back of the paper |

Figure 3.2. Product guidelines

| Video | Window Pane | Worksheet |
|---|---|---|
| • Use VHS or DVD format<br>• Turn in a written plan or storyboard with project<br>• Students will need to arrange their own video recorder or allow teacher at least 3 days notice for use of video recorder<br>• Covers important information about the project<br>• Name must be written on video label | • At least 8.5" x 11"<br>• At least six squares<br>• Each square must include both a picture and words<br>• Name should be recorded on the bottom righthand corner of the front of the window pane | • Must be 8.5" x 11"<br>• Neatly written or typed<br>• Must cover the specific topic or question in detail<br>• Must be creative in design<br>• Must have at least one graphic<br>• An answer key will be turned in with the worksheet |
| **You Be the Person Presentation**<br><br>• Take on the role of the person<br>• Cover at least five important facts about his or her life<br>• Presentation should be 3–5 minutes in length<br>• Script must be turned in prior to the presentation<br>• Should be prepared to answer questions from the audience while in character<br>• Must have props or a costume | | |
| | | |
| | | |

Figure 3.2. Product guidelines

One of the most commonly used products in a language arts classroom is the story map. The story map is a quick and effective way for a student to dissect a story and show that he or she can analyze the important parts of the story. Story maps are an option for approximately one third of the menus provided in this book. Two examples are offered (see Figures 3.3 and 3.4); however, teachers who have a favorite format that students are accustomed to should feel free to use their own.

# Story Map

### Title and Author

### Setting

### Main Characters
With at Least Three Traits for Each

### Supporting Characters
With One Sentence About Why They Are Important

### Problem

### Major Events in the Story

### Solution

Figure 3.3. Story map 1

# Story Map

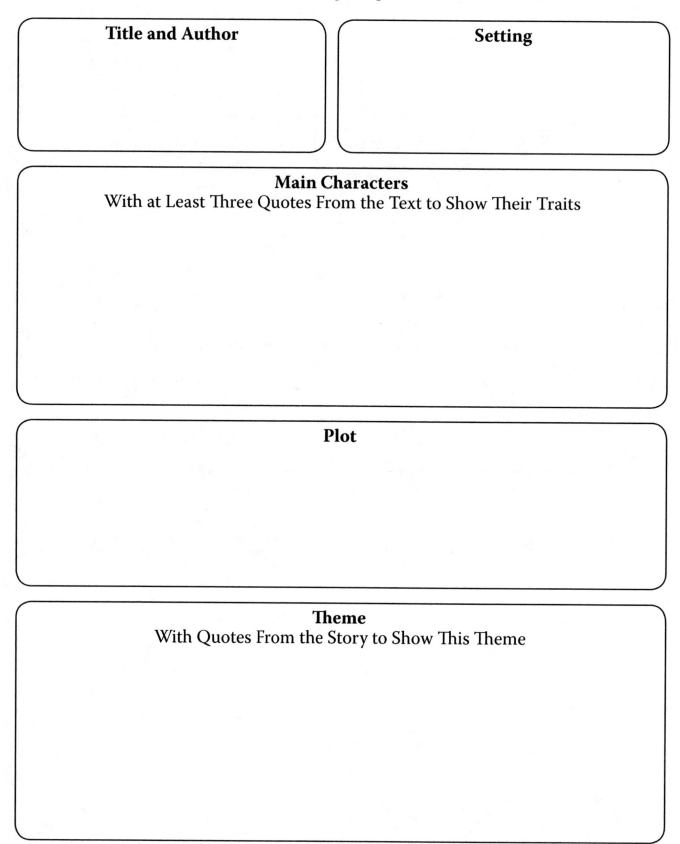

**Title and Author**

**Setting**

**Main Characters**
With at Least Three Quotes From the Text to Show Their Traits

**Plot**

**Theme**
With Quotes From the Story to Show This Theme

Figure 3.4. Story map 2

# CHAPTER 4

# Rubrics

The most common reason teachers feel uncomfortable with menus is the need for equal grading. Teachers often feel it is easier to grade the same type of product made by all of the students, rather than grading a large number of different products, none of which looks like any other. The great equalizer for hundreds of different products is a generic rubric that can cover all of the important qualities of an excellent product.

## All-Purpose Rubric

Figure 4.1 is an example of a rubric that has been classroom tested with various menus. This rubric can be used with any point value activity

Name:_____

# All-Purpose Product Rubric

| Criteria | Excellent Full Credit | Good Half Credit | Poor No Credit | Self |
|---|---|---|---|---|
| **Content:** Is the content of the product well chosen? | Content chosen represents the best choice for the product. Graphics are well chosen and related to content. | Information or graphics are related to content, but are not the best choice for the product. | Information or graphics presented does not appear to be related to topic or task. | |
| **Completeness:** Is everything included in the product? | All information needed is included. Product meets the product criteria and the criteria of the task as stated. | Some important information is missing. Product meets the product criteria and the criteria of the task as stated. | Most important information is missing. The product does not meet the task, or does not meet the product criteria. | |
| **Creativity:** Is the product original? | Presentation of information is from a new perspective. Graphics are original. Product includes an element of fun and interest. | Presentation of information is from a new perspective. Graphics are not original. Product has elements of fun and interest. | There is no evidence of new thoughts or perspectives in the product. | |
| **Correctness:** Is all the information included correct? | All information presented in the product is correct and accurate. | N/A | Any portion of the information presented in the product is incorrect. | |
| **Appropriate Communication:** Is the information in the product well communicated? | All information is neat and easy to read. Product is in appropriate format and shows significant effort. Oral presentations are easy to understand and presented with fluency. | Most of the product is neat and easy to read. Product is in appropriate format and shows significant effort. Oral presentations are easy to understand, with some fluency. | The product is not neat and easy to read or the product is not in the appropriate format. It does not show significant effort. Oral presentation was not fluent or easy to understand. | |
| | | | **Total Grade** | |

Figure 4.1. All-purpose product rubric

presented in a menu. When a menu is presented to students, this rubric can be reproduced on the back of the menu with its guidelines. It can also be given to students to keep in their folder with their product cards so they always know the expectations as they complete projects throughout the school year. The first time students see this rubric, it should be explained in detail, especially the last column titled *self*. It is very important that students self-evaluate their projects. This column can provide a unique perspective of the project as it is being graded. Note: This rubric was designed to be specific enough that students will know the criteria the teacher is seeking, but general enough that they can still be as creative as they like in the creation of their product.

## Student-Taught Lessons and Student Presentation Rubrics

Although the generic rubric can be used for all activities, there are two occasions that seem to warrant a special rubric: student-taught lessons and student presentations. These are unique situations, with many fine details that should be considered separately.

Teachers often would like to allow students to teach their fellow classmates, but are not comfortable with the grading aspect of the assignment. The student-taught lesson rubric helps focus the student on the important aspects of a well-designed lesson, and allows teachers to make the evaluation a little more subjective. The student-taught lesson rubric (see Figure 4.2) included for these menus is appropriate for all levels.

Another area that can be difficult to evaluate is student presentations. The first consideration is that of objectivity. The objectivity can be addressed through a very specific presentation rubric that states the expectations for the speaker. The rubric will need to be discussed before the students begin preparing presentations and various criteria needs to be demonstrated. The second consideration is that of the audience and its interest. It can be frustrating to have to grade 30 presentations when the audience is not paying attention, off task, or tuning out. This can be solved by allowing your audience to be directly involved in the presentation. All of the students have been instructed on the oral presentation rubric (see Figure 4.3), so when they receive their own rubric to give feedback to their classmates, they are quite comfortable with the criteria. Students are asked to rank their classmates on a scale of 1–10 in the areas of content, flow, and the prop they chose to enhance their

## Student-Taught Lesson Grading Rubric          Name _____

| Parts of Lesson | Excellent | Good | Fair | Poor | Self |
|---|---|---|---|---|---|
| **Prepared and Ready:**<br><br>All materials and lesson ready at start of class period, from warm-up to conclusion of lesson. | **10**<br><br>Everything is ready to present. | **6**<br><br>Lesson is present, but small amount of scrambling. | **3**<br><br>Lesson is present, but major scrambling. | **0**<br><br>No lesson ready or missing major components. | |
| **Understanding:**<br><br>Presenter understands the material well. Students understand information presented. | **20**<br><br>Presenter understands; almost all of the students understand information. | **12**<br><br>Presenter understands; 25% of students do not. | **4**<br><br>Presenter understands; 50% of students do not. | **0**<br><br>Presenter is confused. | |
| **Completion:**<br><br>Includes all significant information from section or topic. | **15**<br><br>Includes all important information. | **10**<br><br>Includes most important information. | **2**<br><br>Includes less than 50% of the important information. | **0**<br><br>Information is not related. | |
| **Practice:**<br><br>Includes some way for students to practice or access the information. | **20**<br><br>Practice present, well chosen. | **10**<br><br>Practice present, can be applied effectively. | **5**<br><br>Practice present, not related or best choice. | **0**<br><br>No practice or students are confused. | |
| **Interest/Fun:**<br><br>Most of the class involved, interested, and participating. | **15**<br><br>Everyone interested and participating. | **10**<br><br>75% actively participating. | **5**<br><br>Less than 50% actively participating. | **0**<br><br>Everyone off task. | |
| **Creativity:**<br><br>Information presented in imaginative way. | **20**<br><br>Wow, creative! I never would have thought of that! | **12**<br><br>Good ideas! | **5**<br><br>Some good pieces but general instruction. | **0**<br><br>No creativity; all lecture/ notes/ worksheet. | |
| | | | | **Total Grade:** | |

**Your Topic/Objective:**


**Comments:**


**Don't Forget:**
All copy requests and material requests must be made at least 24 hours in advance.

Figure 4.2. Student-taught lesson grading rubric

presentation (see Figure 4.4). They are also asked to state two things the presenter did well. Although most students understand this should be a positive experience for the presenter, it may want to be reinforced that some notes are not necessary on their peer rankings; for example, if the presenter dropped his or her product and had to pick it up, the presenter knows this and it probably does not need to be noted again. The feedback should be positive and specific, as well. A comment of "Great!" is not what should be recorded; instead, something specific such as "I could hear you speak loudly and clearly throughout the entire presentation," or "You had great graphics!" should be written on the form. These types of comments really make the students take note and feel great about their presentations. The teacher should not be surprised to note that the students often look through all of their classmates' feedback and comments before ever consulting the rubric the teacher completed. Once students have completed a feedback form for a presenter, the forms can then be gathered at the end of each presentation, stapled together, and given to the presenter at the end of the class.

# Oral Presentation Rubric

| | Excellent | Good | Fair | Poor | Self |
|---|---|---|---|---|---|
| **Content— Complete**<br><br>The presentation included everything it should. | **30**<br><br>Presentation included all of the important information about the topic being presented. | **20**<br><br>Presentation covered most of the important information, but one key idea was missing. | **10**<br><br>Presentation covered some of the important information, but more than one key idea was missing. | **0**<br><br>Presentation included some information, but it was trivial or fluff. | |
| **Content—Correct**<br><br>All of the information presented was accurate. | **30**<br><br>All of the information presented was accurate. | **20**<br><br>All of the information presented was correct with a few unintentional errors that were quickly corrected. | **10**<br><br>Most of the information presented was correct, but there were a few errors. | **0**<br><br>The information presented was not correct. | |
| **Content— Consistency**<br><br>Speaker stayed on topic during the presentation. | **10**<br><br>Presenter stayed on topic 100% of the time. | **7**<br><br>Presenter stayed on topic 90–99% of the time. | **4**<br><br>Presenter stayed on topic 80–89% of the time. | **0**<br><br>It was hard to tell what the topic was. | |
| **Prop**<br><br>Speaker had at least one prop that was directly related to the presentation. | **20**<br><br>Presenter had the prop and it complimented the presentation. | **12**<br><br>Presenter had a prop, but it was not the best choice. | **4**<br><br>Presenter had a prop, but there was no clear reason for its choice. | **0**<br><br>No prop. | |
| **Flow**<br><br>Speaker knew the presentation well, so the words were well-spoken and flowed well together. | **10**<br><br>Presentation flowed well. Speaker did not stumble over words. | **7**<br><br>Some flow problems, but they did not distract from information. | **4**<br><br>Some flow problems interrupted presentation; presenter seemed flustered. | **0**<br><br>Constant flow problems; information was not presented in a way it could be understood. | |
| | | | | **Total Grade:** | |

Figure 4.3. Oral presentation rubric

Topic: _____    Student's Name_____

On a scale of 1–10, rate the following areas:

| Content<br>(Depth of information. How well did the speaker know his or her information? Was the information correct? Could the speaker answer questions?) | Your Ranking | Give one specific reason why you gave this number. |
|---|---|---|
| Flow<br>(Did the presentation flow smoothly? Did the speaker appear confident and ready to speak?) | Your Ranking | Give one specific reason why you gave this number. |
| Prop<br>(Did the speaker explain the prop he or she chose? Did the choice seem logical? Was it the best choice?) | Your Ranking | Give one specific reason why you gave this number. |

Comments: Below, write two specific things that you think the presenter did well.

- - - - - - - - - - - - - - - - - - - - - - - - - - - - - - - - - - - - - - - - - - - - - - - - - - - - - - - - -

Topic: _____    Student's Name_____

On a scale of 1–10, rate the following areas:

| Content<br>(Depth of information. How well did the speaker know his or her information? Was the information correct? Could the speaker answer questions?) | Your Ranking | Give one specific reason why you gave this number. |
|---|---|---|
| Flow<br>(Did the presentation flow smoothly? Did the speaker appear confident and ready to speak?) | Your Ranking | Give one specific reason why you gave this number. |
| Prop<br>(Did the speaker explain the prop he or she chose? Did the choice seem logical? Was it the best choice?) | Your Ranking | Give one specific reason why you gave this number. |

Comments: Below, write two specific things that you think the presenter did well.

Figure 4.4. Student feedback rubric

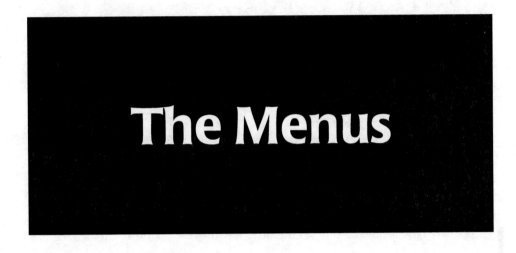

# The Menus

## How to Use the Menu Pages

Each menu in this section has:
- an introduction page for the teacher,
- the content menu,
- any specific guidelines, and
- activities mentioned in the menu.

## Introduction Pages

The introduction pages are meant to provide an overview of each menu. They are divided into five areas.

1. *Objectives covered through the menu and activities.* This area will list all of the objectives that the menu can address. Menus are arranged in such a way that if students complete the guidelines set forth in the instructions for the menu, all of these objectives will be covered.

2. *Materials needed by students for completion.* For each menu, it is expected that the teacher will provide or students will have access to the following materials: lined paper; glue; crayons, colored pencils,

or markers; and blank 8 ½" by 11" white paper. The introduction page also includes a list of additional materials that may be needed by students. Students do have the choice about the menu items they can complete, so it is possible that the teacher will not need all of these materials for every student.

3. *Special notes.* Some menus allow students to choose to present demonstrations, experiments, songs, or PowerPoint presentations to their classmates. This section will give any special tips on managing these student presentations. This section will also share any tips to consider for a specific activity.

4. *Time frame.* Most menus are best used in at least a one-week time frame. Some are better suited to more than 2 weeks. This section will give you an overview about the best time frame for completing the entire menu, as well as options for shorter time periods. If teachers do not have time to devote to an entire menu, they can certainly choose the 1–2-day option for any menu topic students are currently studying.

5. *Suggested forms.* This is a list of the rubrics that should be available for students as the menus are introduced. If a menu has a free-choice option, the appropriate proposal form also will be listed here.

# CHAPTER 5

# Genres

# Fiction

## 2-5-8 Menu

### *Reading Objectives Covered Through This Menu and These Activities*

- Students will read from a variety of genres for pleasure and to acquire information.
- Students will show comprehension by summarizing the story.
- Students will analyze characters, their relationships, and their importance in the story.
- Students will recognize story problems or plot.
- Students will represent textual information by using story maps.

### *Writing Objectives Covered Through This Menu and These Activities*

- Students will support their responses with textual evidence.
- Students will write to inform, explain, describe, or narrate.
- Students will exhibit voice in their writing.

### *Materials Needed by Students for Completion*

- Poster board or large white paper
- Graph paper or Internet access (for crossword puzzle)
- Blank index cards (for recipe card)
- Story map of teacher's choice

### *Time Frame*

- 1–2 weeks—Students are given the menu as the unit is started, and the teacher discusses all of the product options on the menu. As the different options are discussed, students will choose products that add to a total of 10 points. As the lessons progress through the week, the teacher and students refer back to the options associated with the content being taught.
- 1–2 days—The teacher chooses an activity from the menu to use with the entire class.

### *Suggested Forms*

- All-purpose rubric
- Proposal form for point-based projects

Name:_____

# Fiction

**Directions:** Choose two activities from the menu below. The activities must total 10 points. Place a checkmark next to each box to show which activities you will complete. All activities must be completed by

_____.

## 2 Points

☐ Complete a story map for a fictional story of your choice.

☐ Create a quiz addressing what important elements a fictional story should contain.

## 5 Points

☐ Make a recipe for a good fictional story.

☐ Read a fictional book of your choice and create a crossword puzzle about the important elements.

☐ Create a poster to show your favorite fictional character. On the poster, place the character in his or her setting, and surround the character with elements from the story.

☐ Free choice—Prepare a proposal form and submit it to your teacher for approval.

## 8 Points

☐ Write your own fictional short story about someone your age and a problem he or she must solve.

☐ The Book Hall of Fame is taking nominations for the best fictional book ever written. Write a submission for this honor. Describe the book you picked and why it deserves the honor.

```
2
  □ _____
  □ _____
5
  □ _____
  □ _____
  □ _____
  □ _____
8
  □ _____
  □ _____
```

# Tall Tales

## 2-5-8 Menu

### Background Information

All tall tales have similar elements. Tall tales usually include:

- lots of action and exaggerations,
- a main character who faces problems and has to solve them before the end of the tale,
- a main character who is larger than life or has super-human abilities, and
- a tale that is funny.

See the appendix for a book list of popular tall tales.

### Reading Objectives Covered Through This Menu and These Activities

- Students will read from a variety of genres for pleasure and to acquire information.
- Students will distinguish fact from fiction.
- Students will interpret figurative language.
- Students will show comprehension by retelling or acting out events in the story.
- Students will show comprehension by summarizing the story.
- Students will analyze characters, their relationships, and their importance in the story.
- Students will recognize story problems or plot.
- Students will recognize distinguishing features of tall tales.
- Students will make and explain inferences made from the story.
- Students will make predictions based on what is read in the story.

### Writing Objectives Covered Through This Menu and These Activities

- Students will support their responses with textual evidence.
- Students will write to inform, explain, describe, or narrate.
- Students will write to entertain.
- Students will exhibit voice in their writing.
- Students will use vivid language.

### Materials Needed by Students for Completion

- Video camera (for news report)
- Blank index cards (for trading cards)
- Scrapbooking materials

### Time Frame

- 1–2 weeks—Students are given the menu as the unit is started, and the teacher discusses all of the product options on the menu. As the different options are discussed, students will choose products that add to a total of 10 points. As the lessons progress through the week, the teacher and students refer back to the options associated with the content being taught.
- 1–2 days—The teacher chooses an activity from the menu to use with the entire class.

### Suggested Forms

- All-purpose rubric

Name:_____

# Tall Tales

**Directions:** Choose two activities from the menu below. The activities must total 10 points. Place a checkmark next to each box to show which activities you will complete. All activities must be completed by
_____.

---

**2 Points**

❑ Make a mind map to show the important elements found in tall tales.

❑ Make a set of trading cards for the main characters in five tall tales.

---

**5 Points**

❑ Research the character in your tall tale, and create a T-chart to show the parts of the story that were fact and the parts that were fiction.

❑ Create a news report to tell the mighty accomplishments of the main character in your tall tale.

❑ Design an advertisement for your main character and his or her superior skills.

❑ Make a scrapbook that shows the great accomplishments of the main character of your tall tale.

❑ Take your tall tale and break it into parts to show all of the important elements of a tall tale.

---

**8 Points**

❑ Pretend you are a character in your own tall tale. Write five journal entries that tell about your adventures.

❑ Come to class as your favorite tall tale hero. Be prepared to tell a tale of an adventure your classmates may not know.

# Folk Tales

## 2-5-8 Menu

### Background Information

All folk tales have similar elements. Folk tales usually include:

- wishes being granted,
- magical objects used throughout the story,
- animals that talk,
- the use of trickery,
- the number three, or
- a poor person becoming rich.

Folk tales usually follow a predictable pattern. The stories often start very quickly so children are drawn into the story with ease. The characters are simplistic, and as they progress through the tale, the plots often seem predictable. Most problems do get resolved in a happy ending. See the appendix for a book list of popular folk tales.

### Reading Objectives Covered Through This Menu and These Activities

- Students will read from a variety of genres for pleasure and to acquire information.
- Students will interpret figurative language and multiple meaning words.
- Students will show comprehension by retelling or acting out events in the story.
- Students will show comprehension by summarizing the story.
- Students will recognize story problems or plot.
- Students will represent textual information by using story maps.
- Students will compare one literary work with another.
- Students will recognize distinguishing features of folk tales.
- Students will compare different forms of a story (written versus performed).

### Writing Objectives Covered Through This Menu and These Activities

- Students will write to inform, explain, describe, or narrate.
- Students will write to entertain.
- Students will revise drafts.
- Students will use vivid language.

## Materials Needed by Students for Completion

- Poster board or large white paper
- Story map of teacher's choice
- Shoe boxes (for dioramas)

## Time Frame

- 1–2 weeks—Students are given the menu as the unit is started, and the teacher discusses all of the product options on the menu. As the different options are discussed, students will choose products that add to a total of 10 points. As the lessons progress through the week, the teacher and students refer back to the options associated with the content being taught.
- 1–2 days—The teacher chooses an activity from the menu to use with the entire class.

## Suggested Forms

- All-purpose rubric
- $1 contract (for diorama)

Name:_____

# Folk Tales

**Directions:** Choose two activities from the menu below. The activities must total 10 points. Place a checkmark next to each box to show which activities you will complete. All activities must be completed by _____.

---

**2 Points**

❒ Complete a story map for your folk tale.

❒ Make a poster that shows the elements found in folk tales.

---

**5 Points**

❒ Design a survey to discover your classmates' favorite folk tale. Record your data and design a way to present it.

❒ Design a diorama that shows the setting and characters in your folk tale.

❒ Make a Venn diagram that compares folk tales to tall tales.

❒ Create a book cover for a folk tale your choice.

---

**8 Points**

❒ Turn one of your favorite folk tales into a play. Submit your script to your teacher.

❒ Create your own folk tale. Include a story map and rough draft of your ideas.

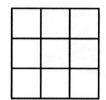

# Alphabet Books

## Tic-Tac-Toe Menu

See the appendix for a book list of popular alphabet books.

### _Reading Objectives Covered Through This Menu and These Activities_
- Students will compare one literary work with another.
- Students will draw conclusions and make predictions on what is read in the story.

### _Writing Objectives Covered Through This Menu and These Activities_
- Students will write to express, develop, reflect, or problem solve.
- Students will write to inform, explain, describe, or narrate.
- Students will write to entertain.
- Students will exhibit voice in their writing.
- Students will use vivid language.

### _Materials Needed by Students for Completion_
- Materials for board games (e.g., folders, colored cards)
- Materials for puppets
- Alphabet cube handout

### _Time Frame_
- 2 weeks—Students are given the menu as the unit is started and the guidelines and point expectations are discussed. As lessons are taught throughout the unit, students and the teacher can refer back to the options associated with that topic. The teacher will go over all of the options for the topic being covered and have students place check-marks in the boxes next to the activities they are most interested in completing. As teaching continues during next 2 weeks, activities chosen and completed should make a column or row.
- 1 week—At the start of the unit, the teacher chooses the three activities he or she feels are most valuable for the students. Stations can be set up in the classroom. These three activities are available for student choice throughout the week, as regular instruction takes place.
- 1–2 days—The teacher chooses an activity from the menu to use with the entire class.

## *Suggested Forms*

- All-purpose rubric
- Proposal forms
- $1 contract (for puppet)

# Alphabet Menu Book

| | | |
|---|---|---|
| ☐ *Write a Review*<br>Read one of Jerry Pallotta's alphabet books. Look at the drawings, as well as the words, as you read. Write a review of the book. Address whether other students would enjoy it and why or why not. | ☐ *Create a Song or Rap*<br>Convert an alphabet book of your choice into a song or rap. Share your new song with your classmates. | ☐ *Create a Book*<br>Create an alphabet book of books. Think of all the books you have enjoyed and create an alphabet book with one page for each book. Choose your illustrations carefully! |
| ☐ *Create Your Own Book*<br>Think of a topic you enjoy in science. Create an alphabet book for this topic. | ☐ **Free Choice**<br><br>(Fill out your proposal form before beginning the free choice!) | ☐ *Make a Puppet*<br>After choosing an alphabet book, create a puppet distinctive to the book that could be used to narrate your chosen book. |
| ☐ *Design a Board Game*<br>Create an ABC-themed board game. Your question and activity cards should have a rhyming theme. | ☐ *Create an Acrostic*<br>Choose a topic from one of your classes that interests you. Create an acrostic for the topic. Use this to create your own alphabet book. | ☐ *Create a Cube*<br>Using the cube format, create a math-based alphabet cube. Each side should have a letter, a drawing, and information about a math idea associated with that letter. |

Check the boxes you plan to complete. They should form a tic-tac-toe across or down. All products are due by: _____.

# Math Alphabet Cube

Complete an alphabet cube for math words. Use this pattern or create your own cube. Each side of this cube should have a letter, a drawing, and information about a math idea associated with that letter.

# Science Fiction

## 2-5-8 Menu

### *Reading Objectives Covered Through This Menu and These Activities*

- Students will show comprehension by summarizing the story.
- Students will analyze characters, their relationships, and their importance in the story.
- Students will represent textual information by using story maps.
- Students will compare one literary genre with another.
- Students will recognize distinguishing features of science fiction.

### *Writing Objectives Covered Through This Menu and These Activities*

- Students will support their responses with textual evidence.
- Students will write to express, develop, reflect, or problem solve.
- Students will write to inform, explain, describe, or narrate.
- Students will write to entertain.
- Students will exhibit voice in their writing.

### *Materials Needed by Students for Completion*

- Materials for board games (e.g., folders, colored cards, etc.)
- Story map of teacher's choice

### *Time Frame*

- 1–2 weeks—Students are given the menu as the unit is started, and the teacher discusses all of the product options on the menu. As the different options are discussed, students will choose products that add to a total of 10 points. As the lessons progress through the week, the teacher and students refer back to the options associated with the content being taught.
- 1–2 days—The teacher chooses an activity from the menu to use with the entire class.

### *Suggested Forms*

- All-purpose rubric

# Science Fiction

**Directions:** Choose two activities from the menu below. The activities must total 10 points. Place a checkmark next to each box to show which activities you will complete. All activities must be completed by _____.

## 2 Points

❒ Create a mind map that shows all of the important elements found in a science fiction story.

❒ Make an acrostic for the word *science fiction*. Use a phrase to describe this genre for each letter.

## 5 Points

❒ Take your favorite science fiction story and make a board game with the same theme.

❒ Make an advertisement for a science fiction book of your choice.

❒ Make a Venn diagram to compare and contrast science fiction stories with folk tales.

❒ Take your favorite science fiction character and show his or her next adventure using a cartoon format.

## 8 Points

❒ Develop a lesson that teaches your classmates how to write a science fiction story.

❒ Write your own science fiction story set in the future. Include a story map that shows your prewriting, as well as your rough draft.

# Mysteries

## Tic-Tac-Toe Menu

### *Reading Objectives Covered Through This Menu and These Activities*

- Students will show comprehension by retelling or acting out events in the story.
- Students will show comprehension by summarizing the story.
- Students will recognize story problems or plot.
- Students will represent textual information by using story maps.
- Students will recognize distinguishing features of mysteries.

### *Writing Objectives Covered Through This Menu and These Activities*

- Students will write to inform, explain, describe, or narrate.
- Students will write to entertain.
- Students will exhibit voice in their writing.

### *Materials Needed by Students for Completion*

- Materials for board games (e.g., folders, colored cards, etc.)
- Video camera (for commercial)
- Microsoft PowerPoint or other slideshow software
- Blank index cards (for card game)
- Story map of teacher's choice

### *Time Frame*

- 2 weeks—Students are given the menu as the unit is started and the guidelines and point expectations are discussed. As lessons are taught throughout the unit, students and the teacher can refer back to the options associated with that topic. The teacher will go over all of the options for the topic being covered and have students place check-marks in the boxes next to the activities they are most interested in completing. As teaching continues during next 2 weeks, activities chosen and completed should make a column or row.
- 1 week—At the start of the unit, the teacher chooses the three activities he or she feels are most valuable for the students. Stations can be set up in the classroom. These three activities are available for student choice throughout the week, as regular instruction takes place.
- 1–2 days—The teacher chooses an activity from the menu to use with the entire class.

*Suggested Forms*

- All-purpose rubric
- Proposal forms

Name:_____

# Mysteries

| ☐ Create a Board Game | ☐ You Be the Person Presentation | ☐ Design a Book Cover |
|---|---|---|
| Create a board game with a mystery-based theme. Be creative in your choice of pieces, game cards, and rules. | Research a mystery author. Prepare a "You be the Person Presentation" for your classmates. Be prepared to answer questions about your life and the books that you write. | Read a mystery of your choice. Create a new book cover for the book that you choose. |
| ☐ Complete a Story Map | ☐ Free Choice | ☐ Get Ready for the News! |
| After you have read your mystery, complete the story map. | (Fill out your proposal form before beginning the free choice!) | Your favorite mystery novel is being re-released to the public. Prepare a news report to discuss the book and cover the excitement of the crowds waiting to buy the book. |
| ☐ Prepare a Commercial | ☐ Create a Recipe | ☐ Create Trading Cards |
| Your favorite mystery novel is being re-released to the public. Prepare a commercial for the book that includes teasers to encourage people to read the book, but don't give away the ending! | Think about all of the elements that make a good mystery. Create a recipe card that shows the ingredients of a well-written mystery. | Think of at least six popular mysteries. Create a trading card for each book. Include the main characters and a description of the plot, but don't give away the ending! |

Check the boxes you plan to complete. They should form a tic-tac-toe across or down. All products are due by: _____.

# Plays

## 2-5-8 Menu

### *Reading Objectives Covered Through This Menu and These Activities*

- Students will show comprehension by retelling or acting out events in the story.
- Students will show comprehension by summarizing the story.
- Students will represent textual information by using story maps.
- Students will compare different forms of a story (written versus performed).

### *Writing Objectives Covered Through This Menu and These Activities*

- Students will write to inform, explain, describe, or narrate.
- Students will write to entertain.
- Students will exhibit voice in their writing.
- Students will revise drafts.

### *Materials Needed by Students for Completion*

- Poster board or large white paper
- Cube template
- Story map of teacher's choice
- Materials for making puppets

### *Time Frame*

- 1–2 weeks—Students are given the menu as the unit is started, and the teacher discusses all of the product options on the menu. As the different options are discussed, students will choose products that add to a total of 10 points. As the lessons progress through the week, the teacher and students refer back to the options associated with the content being taught.
- 1–2 days—The teacher chooses an activity from the menu to use with the entire class.

### *Suggested Forms*

- All-purpose rubric
- $1 contract (for puppet)

Name:_____

# Plays

**Directions:** Choose two activities from the menu below. The activities must total 10 points. Place a checkmark next to each box to show which activities you will complete. All activities must be completed by _____.

---

**2 Points**

❏ Read a play of your choice. Complete the story map of the play you read.

❏ Complete The Play Cube.

---

**5 Points**

❏ Make your own puppet for a character in the play you are reading.

❏ Research a theater where plays are performed or have been performed in the past. Discover what was special about their structures. Present your finding on a poster.

❏ Read a play of your choice. Review the play in a newspaper article and include specific reasons for why you like or dislike the play.

❏ Choose one of your favorite fictional stories. Change this story into a play.

---

**8 Points**

❏ Write your own play to perform for your classmates. (Ask some of your classmates to help you perform your play.)

❏ Make a puppet show with at least two characters to share with your classmates.

# The Play Cube

Complete the cube for the play you have read. Use this pattern or create your own cube. Respond to the questions on each side to analyze your play in depth.

Summarize your play in one sentence.

List all of the characters in your play.

What were the major events that occurred in your play?

Describe the setting.

What was your favorite part of the play?

Which character was most important in the play? Why?

# Poetry

## Tic-Tac-Toe Menu

### Reading Objectives Covered Through This Menu and These Activities

- Students will compare one literary work with another.
- Students will recognize distinguishing features of cinquain, diamante, and haiku poems.

### Writing Objectives Covered Through This Menu and These Activities

- Students will write to express their feelings.
- Students will write to inform, explain, describe, or narrate.
- Students will write to entertain.
- Students will exhibit voice in their writing.
- Students will use vivid language.

### Materials Needed by Students for Completion

- Poster board or large white paper
- Cube template
- Information sheets on different types of poems.

### Time Frame

- 2 weeks—Students are given the menu as the unit is started and the guidelines and point expectations are discussed. As lessons are taught throughout the unit, students and the teacher can refer back to the options associated with that topic. The teacher will go over all of the options for the topic being covered and have students place checkmarks in the boxes next to the activities they are most interested in completing. As teaching continues over next 2 weeks, activities chosen and completed should make a column or row.
- 1 week—At the start of the unit, the teacher chooses the three activities he or she feels are most valuable for the students. Stations can be set up in the classroom. These three activities are available for student choice throughout the week, as regular instruction takes place.
- 1–2 days—The teacher chooses an activity from the menu to use with the entire class.

### Suggested Forms

- All-purpose rubric
- Proposal forms

# Poetry

| | | |
|---|---|---|
| ☐ *Create a Cube*<br>Create a poem cube with different stanzas on each side that when rolled could create a poem. | ☐ *Design a Poster*<br>Research the history of the haiku poem. Make a poster that details your research and include three examples of this type of poem. | ☐ *Write a Book*<br>Create a book of poetry with examples from at least three different poetry types (e.g., diamante, cinquain, haiku, name poems, free verse) |
| ☐ *Create a Poem*<br>Write a poem about your classroom or classmates. Use either the diamante or the cinquain format. | ☐ *Free Choice*<br>(Fill out your proposal form before beginning the free choice!) | ☐ *Develop Your Own Song*<br>Choose one of your favorite poems and change it into a song or rap. Be prepared to share your creation with your classmates. |
| ☐ *Illustrate a Poem*<br>Choose a poem from one of Shel Silverstein's poetry books. Create your own illustration for the poem you chose. | ☐ *Your Own Poetry Challenge*<br>Write a poem in a format of your choice. | ☐ *Design a Poster*<br>Gather information on how diamante, cinquain, and haiku poems are written. Create a poster that shows each poem's structure, as well as examples of each. |

Check the boxes you plan to complete. They should form a tic-tac-toe across or down. All products are due by: _____.

# Poetry Cube

Complete a poetry cube. Each side of the cube should have phrases or stanzas. It should be designed so that when rolled three times, a poem could be written with what was rolled. Use this pattern or create your own cube.

Name:_____

# Types of Poems

## *Cinquain Poem*

Line 1—a one-word title (usually two syllables)

Line 2—two words that describe your title (usually four syllables)

Line 3—three verbs or a three-word phase that describes an action relating to your title (usually six syllables)

Line 4—a four-word phrase that describes a feeling related to your title (usually eight syllables)

Line 5—one word that is another word for your title (usually two syllables)

Chadwick

Funny Puppy

Running, Jumping, Barking

Chadwick—A Magnificent Dog

Scottie

## *Diamante Poem*

Line 1—a one-word noun

Line 2—two adjectives that describe the noun in Line 1

Line 3—three action verbs relating to noun in Line 1

Line 4—four nouns that both words in Line 1 and Line 7 have in common

Line 5— three action verbs relating to noun in Line 7

Line 6—two adjectives that describes the noun in Line 7

Line 7—one-word noun that is opposite of the noun in Line 1

Sun

Warm, Bright

Shines, Heats, Creates

Weather, Beach, Children, Outdoors

Cools, Waters, Feeds

Fresh, Welcome

Rain

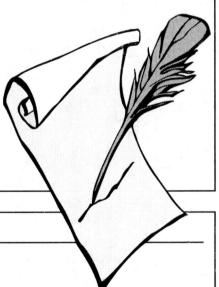

## *Haiku Poem*

Line 1—a five-syllable line

Line 2—a seven-syllable line

Line 3—a five-syllable line

Rain, it softly falls

Trees thirst and drink greedily

The forest sings out.

# Nonfiction

## Tic-Tac-Toe Menu

### *Reading Objectives Covered Through This Menu and These Activities*
- Students will show comprehension by summarizing the information in the book.
- Students will distinguish fact from opinion.

### *Writing Objectives Covered Through This Menu and These Activities*
- Students will write to express, develop, reflect, or problem solve.
- Students will write to inform, explain, describe, or narrate.
- Students will revise drafts.

### *Materials Needed by Students for Completion*
- Materials for student created models
- Magazines (for collage)
- Video camera (for commercial)

### *Time Frame*
- 2 weeks—Students are given the menu as the unit is started and the guidelines and point expectations are discussed. As lessons are taught throughout the unit, students and the teacher can refer back to the options associated with that topic. The teacher will go over all of the options for the topic being covered and have students place check-marks in the boxes next to the activities they are most interested in completing. As teaching continues during next 2 weeks, activities chosen and completed should make a column or row.
- 1 week—At the start of the unit, the teacher chooses the three activities he or she feels are most valuable for the students. Stations can be set up in the classroom. These three activities are available for student choice throughout the week, as regular instruction takes place.
- 1–2 days—The teacher chooses an activity from the menu to use with the entire class.

### *Suggested Forms*
- All-purpose rubric
- Proposal forms

# Nonfiction

| | | |
|---|---|---|
| ☐ *Prepare a Speech*<br>Choose one topic in science or social studies that interests you. After researching more information on the topic, prepare a speech for your class on your findings. | ☐ *Create a Brochure*<br>Think of your favorite pastime or hobby. Create a brochure that explains your hobby, why people might be interested in doing it, and how they could get involved. | ☐ *Create a Collage*<br>Using magazines, create a collage of pictures that represents your personality. Write a paragraph to describe the collage and why you chose the pictures. |
| ☐ *Design a Model Bedroom*<br>Develop a model of your dream bedroom. Write a few paragraphs to go with the model describing the details of your model. | ☐ **Free Choice**<br>(Fill out your proposal form before beginning the free choice!) | ☐ *Create a Commercial*<br>You have invented a new product. Create a commercial for your product. It should explain how to use the product and its benefits. Include a script with your commercial. |
| ☐ *Create a Book Cover*<br>Visit your library and find a book that discusses a hobby you enjoy. After reading the book, create a book cover that could be used for this book. | ☐ *Write a Letter*<br>Choose a book about a place you would like to visit. After reading the book, write a letter to your family describing your trip and the sights you visited. | ☐ *Prepare a Research Paper*<br>Choose a topic you would like to investigate further. Present your topic to your teacher for approval and prepare a research paper with the information you have found. |

Check the boxes you plan to complete. They should form a tic-tac-toe across or down. All products are due by: _____.

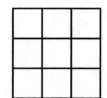

# Biographies

## Tic-Tac-Toe Menu

*Reading Objectives Covered Through This Menu and These Activities*
- Students will show comprehension by retelling or acting out events in the biography.
- Students will show comprehension by summarizing the events in the life of the subject of their biography.
- Students will analyze subjects, their relationships, and their importance in the biography.
- Students will draw conclusions and make prediction on what is read in the book.

*Writing Objectives Covered Through This Menu and These Activities*
- Students will write to inform, explain, describe, or narrate.
- Students will exhibit voice in their writing.
- Students will revise drafts.

*Materials Needed by Students for Completion*
- Microsoft PowerPoint or other slideshow software
- Materials for three-dimensional timeline
- Scrapbooking materials

*Time Frame*
- 2 weeks—Students are given the menu as the unit is started and the guidelines and point expectations are discussed. As lessons are taught throughout the unit, students and the teacher can refer back to the options associated with that topic. The teacher will go over all of the options for the topic being covered and have students place checkmarks in the boxes next to the activities they are most interested in completing. As teaching continues during next 2 weeks, activities chosen and completed should make a column or row.
- 1 week—At the start of the unit, the teacher chooses the three activities he or she feels are most valuable for the students. Stations can be set up in the classroom. These three activities are available for student choice throughout the week, as regular instruction takes place.
- 1–2 days—The teacher chooses an activity from the menu to use with the entire class.

*Suggested Forms*

- All-purpose rubric
- Proposal forms

Name:_____

# Biographies

| | | |
|---|---|---|
| ☐ *Create a Timeline*<br>Choose 10 significant events in the life of the person in the biography. Using these dates, create a three-dimensional timeline of their life. | ☐ *Design a Cereal Box*<br>Famous athletes are not the only people who can be featured on cereal boxes. After reading your biography, design a cereal box for your person. | ☐ *Create a Book Cover*<br>Research an important person from history. Make a book cover that could be used for his or her autobiography. |
| ☐ *Design a Scrapbook*<br>After researching a famous person of your choice, think about the significant events in their life. Create a scrapbook about their life accomplishments. | ☐ **Free Choice**<br>(Fill out your proposal form before beginning the free choice!) | ☐ *You Be the Person Presentation*<br>Prepare a "You Be the Person Presentation" for your classmates. Be prepared to discuss your life and answer questions from your classmates. |
| ☐ *Create a PowerPoint Presentation*<br>Create a list of 10 people you view as being highly important. Choose one and read his or her biography. Create a PowerPoint presentation about his or her life and accomplishments. | ☐ *Write a Letter*<br>Write a letter to send to a famous person asking him or her about his or her life and accomplishments. Research the famous person before composing the letter so you are knowledgeable in your questions. | ☐ *Write an Autobiography*<br>Write an autobiography about your life and your accomplishments. |

Check the boxes you plan to complete. They should form a tic-tac-toe across or down. All products are due by: _____.

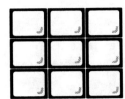

# Genres

## Game Show Menu

### *Reading Objectives Covered Through This Menu and These Activities*

- Students will interpret figurative language and multiple meaning words.
- Students will show comprehension by retelling or acting out events in the story.
- Students will show comprehension by summarizing the story.
- Students will analyze characters, their relationships, and their importance in the story.
- Students will recognize story problems or plot.
- Students will recognize distinguishing features of familiar genres.
- Students will compare different forms of a story (written versus performed).
- Students will make and explain inferences made from the story.
- Students will draw conclusions and make predictions on what is read in the story.

### *Writing Objectives Covered Through This Menu and These Activities*

- Students will write to express, develop, reflect, or problem solve.
- Students will write to inform, explain, describe, or narrate.
- Students will write to entertain.
- Students will exhibit voice in their writing.
- Students will revise drafts.
- Students will use vivid language.

### *Materials Needed by Students for Completion*

- Magazines (for collage)
- Coat hangers (for mobile)
- Index cards (for mobile)
- String (for mobile)
- Materials for the museum exhibit

### *Time Frame*

- 2–3 weeks—Students are given the menu as the unit is started and the guidelines and point expectations are discussed. As lessons are taught throughout the unit, students and the teacher can refer back to the options associated with that topic. The teacher will go over all of the options for the topic being covered and have students place checkmarks in the boxes next to the activities they are most interested in completing. As teaching continues during next 2–3 weeks, activities are discussed, chosen, and submitted for grading.

- 1 week—At the start of the unit, the teacher chooses the three activities he or she feels are most valuable for the students. Stations can be set up in the classroom. These three activities are available for student choice throughout the week, as regular instruction takes place.
- 1–2 days—The teacher chooses an activity from the menu to use with the entire class.

### Suggested Forms

- All-purpose rubric
- Proposal form for point-based projects

# Guidelines for Game Show Menu

- You must choose at least one activity from each topic area.
- You may not do more than two activities in any one topic area for credit. (You are, of course, welcome to do more than two for your own investigation.)
- Grading will be ongoing, so turn in products as you complete them.
- All free-choice proposals must be turned in and approved *prior* to working on that free choice.
- You must earn 120 points for a 100%. You may earn extra credit up to _____ points.
- You must show your plan for completion by: _____.

# Genres

| Folk Tales | Tall Tales | Mystery | Poetry | Nonfiction | Biographies | Points for Each Level |
|---|---|---|---|---|---|---|
| ☐ Make a mind map that shows the parts of your folk tale. (10 pts.) | ☐ Create a mobile that shows the important parts of your favorite tall tale. (10 pts.) | ☐ Create a postage stamp for your favorite mystery. (15 pts.) | ☐ Recite your favorite poem for the class. It should have at least six lines. (10 pts.) | ☐ Create a collage of pictures related to a nonfiction topic of your choice. (10 pts.) | ☐ Make a timeline showing 5–8 important events from the subject's life. (15 pts.) | 10–15 points |
| ☐ Pretend that you are one of the characters in your folk tale. Retell the folk tale from your point of view using expressive language. (20 pts.) | ☐ Write a newspaper article documenting the adventures of a tall-tale character. (25 pts.) | ☐ Brainstorm ideas that could be used in solving mysteries. Develop a handout for other students to use when solving mysteries. (20 pts.) | ☐ Write and illustrate your own haiku poem. (25 pts.) | ☐ Use facts from a nonfiction book to create a museum exhibit. Include a written description of the objects or photos. (20 pts.) | ☐ Write a journal entry about an important life lesson you learned from reading about an individual and how it will help you in the future. (25 pts.) | 20–25 points |
| ☐ Write a script for the movie version of the folk tale. Think about the props you would need and the actions of the actors when they perform it. (30 pts.) | ☐ Write the next great adventure that would happen in your character's life. (30 pts.) | ☐ Choose a topic in history or science and write your own mystery based upon this topic. (30 pts.) | ☐ Decide which type of poem is easiest to create. Write two examples of this poem with a brief explanation about why you chose this type and why it is the easiest to create. (30 pts.) | ☐ Write a song or rap about a nonfiction topic. It needs to include at least 10 details about the topic. (30 pts.) | ☐ Come to class as the person in your biography. Share the top two ways you have impacted the world and made it a better place. (30 pts.) | 30 points |
| Free Choice (prior approval) (25–50 pts.) | Free Choice (prior approval) (25–50 pts.) | Free Choice (prior approval) (25–50 pts.) | Free Choice (prior approval) (25–50 pts.) | Free Choice (prior approval) (25–50 pts.) | Free Choice (prior approval) (25–50 pts.) | 25–50 points |
| Total: | Total: | Total: | Total: | Total: | Total: | Total Grade: |

# CHAPTER 6

# The Novels

This section has novels usually chosen for study at various grade levels. The novels were selected based on their interest for all students, as well as that fact that each is from different a different genre. They have been put in order by reading level, although some students may enjoy reading a book below or above their actual reading level.

# Mr. Popper's Penguins

## List Menu

In *Mr. Popper's Penguins*, Mr. Popper, a painter, expresses an interest in Admiral Drake's expedition and his encounters with penguins. Admiral Drake surprises him with a penguin of his very own. The adventures continue as the Poppers decide how to keep the penguin happy in their warm climate. After many adventures, the Poppers end up with a large family of penguins that help them completely change their lives.

### Reading Objectives Covered Through This Menu and These Activities
- Students will show comprehension by retelling or acting out events in the story.
- Students will show comprehension by summarizing the story.
- Students will analyze characters, their relationships, and their importance in the story.
- Students will recognize story problems or plot.
- Students will make and explain inferences made from the story.
- Students will draw conclusions and make predictions on what is read in the story.
- Students will distinguish fact from opinion.

### Writing Objectives Covered Through This Menu and These Activities
- Students will write to express, develop, reflect, or problem solve.
- Students will write to inform, explain, describe, or narrate.
- Students will write to entertain.
- Students will exhibit voice in their writing.

### Materials Needed by Students for Completion
- *Mr. Popper's Penguins* by Richard Atwater
- Magazines (for collage)
- Coat hangers (for mobile)
- Index cards (for mobile)
- String (for mobile)
- Microsoft PowerPoint or other slideshow software
- Blank index cards (for trading cards)
- Shoe boxes (for dioramas)
- Maps of the world

### Time Frame

- 1–2 weeks—Students are given the menu as the unit is started and the guidelines and point expectations are discussed. Because this menu covers one topic in depth, the teacher will go over all of the options on the menu and have students place checkmarks in the boxes next to the activities they are most interested in completing. Once the students have placed checkmarks next to the activities they are interested in, teachers will set aside a few moments to sign the agreement at the bottom of the page with each student. As instruction continues, activities are completed by students and submitted for grading.
- 1–2 days—The teacher chooses an activity from an objective to use with the entire class during that lesson time.

### Suggested Forms

- All-purpose rubric
- Proposal form for point-based projects
- $1 contract (for diorama)

Name:_____

# Mr. Popper's Penguins Challenge Investigation

## Guidelines:

1. You may complete as many of the activities listed as you would like within the time period given.
2. You may choose any combination of activities.
3. Your goal is 100 points. You may earn up to _____ points in extra credit.
4. You may be as creative as you like within the guidelines listed below.
5. You must show your plan to your teacher by _____.
6. Activities may be turned in at any time during the working time period. They will be graded and recorded on this sheet as you continue to work, so keep it safe!

| Plan to Do | Activity to Complete | Point Value | Date Completed | Points Earned |
|---|---|---|---|---|
| | Research the types of penguins found at the South Pole and create a PowerPoint presentation about these penguins to share with your class. | 25 | | |
| | Create a diorama of your favorite stage performance the penguins had in this story. | 15 | | |
| | At the end of the story, Mr. Popper had to make a decision. Write a editorial newspaper article about his decision and whether you agree or not. | 30 | | |
| | Research the famous names Mr. Popper chose for his male penguins and create a scrapbook for one of these people. | 25 | | |
| | Mr. Popper wrote a letter to Admiral Drake about his expedition. Choose someone who is doing something you are interested in and write him or her a letter telling him or her what you find interesting about his or her work. | 25 | | |
| | Create a mobile with both facts and examples of fiction about penguins found in the story. | 20 | | |
| | Mr. Popper's Penguins were selected to advertise Owens Oceanic Shrimp. Think of another product we have in our stores that the penguins could advertise and develop the advertisement. | 20 | | |
| | On a map, locate the area of the world where penguins live. Mark each area with the type of penguin found there. | 15 | | |
| | Research Admiral Drake's expedition through Antarctica. Come to class as Admiral Drake prepared to talk about your adventures. | 25 | | |
| | Write a journal entry from Captain Cook's point of view that talks about his first day with the Poppers. | 30 | | |
| | Create a set of trading cards for each of the penguins, including information on their likes and dislikes. | 20 | | |
| | Free choice: Must be outlined on a proposal form and approved before beginning work. | Up to 30 | | |
| | **Total number of points you are planning to earn.** | | **Total points earned:** | |

I am planning to complete _____ activities that could earn up to a total of _____ points.

Teacher's initials _____ Student's signature _____

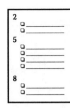

## *Be a Perfect Person in Just Three Days!*

## 2-5-8 Menu

As Milo was searching for a book in the library, a book entitled *Be a Perfect Person in Just Three Days!* fell on his head. Written by a strangely dressed Dr. Silverfish, it outlines the three steps to becoming perfect. As Milo completes the strange steps, he learns what it means to really be perfect.

### Reading Objectives Covered Through This Menu and These Activities

- Students will show comprehension by summarizing the story.
- Students will analyze characters, their relationships, and their importance in the story.
- Students will represent textual information by using story maps.
- Students will judge the internal consistency of logic of stories and text.
- Students will make and explain inferences made from the story.

### Writing Objectives Covered Through This Menu and These Activities

- Students will write to express, develop, reflect, or problem solve.
- Students will write to inform, explain, describe, or narrate.
- Students will revise drafts.

### Materials Needed by Students for Completion

- *Be a Perfect Person in Just Three Days!* by Stephen Manes
- Poster board or large white paper
- Story map of teacher's choice

### Time Frame

- 1–2 weeks—Students are given the menu as the unit is started, and the teacher discusses all of the product options on the menu. As the different options are discussed, students will choose products that add to a total of 10 points. As the lessons progress through the week, the teacher and students refer back to the options associated with the content being taught.
- 1–2 days—The teacher chooses an activity from the menu to use with the entire class.

### Suggested Forms

- All-purpose rubric
- Proposal form for point-based projects

## *Be a Perfect Person in Just Three Days!*

**Directions:** Choose two activities from the menu below. The activities must total 10 points. Place a checkmark next to each box to show which activities you will complete. All activities must be completed by _____.

---

### 2 Points

❒ Complete a story map for *Be a Perfect Person in Just Three Days!*

❒ Free choice—Prepare a proposal form and submit it to your teacher for approval.

---

### 5 Points

❒ Write your own recipe for how to be perfect. Try to be as creative as Dr. Silverfish.

❒ Create a perfection poster. This poster should show what a person would not need if they were perfect. Write a small caption by each item to tell why it would not be needed.

❒ Make an acrostic for the word *perfect*. Use a meaningful phrase for each letter of the word.

❒ What was the most important thing Milo learned from reading his book? Come to class as Milo and present a speech about what he learned and what it means to be perfect.

❒ Create an advertisement that Dr. Silverfish might use to sell *Be a Perfect Person in Just Three Days!*

---

### 8 Points

❒ Create your own book on being perfect. Think about the steps that people should go through to become more "perfect" people.

❒ Not being perfect is sometimes the exact right thing to be. Think of a time when you were not exactly perfect and things turned out well. Write about your experience, giving details about how not being perfect actually made the experience better.

# The Whipping Boy

## 2-5-8 Menu

In *The Whipping Boy*, Prince Brat, who is appropriately named, is always in trouble. It is unacceptable to spank the prince, so Jemmy, an orphan taken from the streets, is always brought forth when Prince Brat needs to be punished. Jemmy decides to run away, but ends up being accompanied by the Prince. They have many adventures, including being kidnapped, Jemmy being mistaken for the prince (and the prince for Jemmy), and traveling through the sewers. Lessons are learned on the parts of both young men.

### *Reading Objectives Covered Through This Menu and These Activities*

- Students will show comprehension by retelling or acting out events in the story.
- Students will show comprehension by summarizing the story.
- Students will analyze characters, their relationships, and their importance in the story.
- Students will recognize story problems or plot.
- Students will compare different forms of a story (written versus performed).
- Students will make and explain inferences made from the story.
- Students will draw conclusions and make predictions on what is read in the story.

### *Writing Objectives Covered Through This Menu and These Activities*

- Students will write to express, develop, reflect, or problem solve.
- Students will write to inform, explain, describe, or narrate.
- Students will write to entertain.
- Students will exhibit voice in their writing.

### *Materials Needed by Students for Completion*

- *The Whipping Boy* by Sid Fleischman
- Video camera (for news report)
- Microsoft PowerPoint or other slideshow software
- Shoe boxes (for dioramas)
- Cube template

## Time Frame

- 1–2 weeks—Students are given the menu as the unit is started, and the teacher discusses all of the product options on the menu. As the different options are discussed, students will choose products that add to a total of 10 points. As the lessons progress through the week, the teacher and students refer back to the options associated with the content being taught.
- 1–2 days—The teacher chooses an activity from the menu to use with the entire class.

## Suggested Forms

- All-purpose rubric
- Student-taught lesson rubric
- Proposal form for point-based projects
- $1 contract (for diorama)

Name:_____

## *The Whipping Boy*

**Directions:** Choose two activities from the menu below. The activities must total 10 points. Place a checkmark next to each box to show which activities you will complete. All activities must be completed by

_____.

---

### 2 Points

❑ Complete a Venn diagram that compares Jemmy and Prince Brat.

❑ Make a diorama for your favorite part of the story.

---

### 5 Points

❑ In this story, Jemmy proves many times that he is a very intelligent boy. Complete a cube by finding six examples from the text that prove this.

❑ This story is set in the Middle Ages in England. Research this period of time and create a PowerPoint presentation that shares information about the people who lived during this time and their living conditions.

❑ The King sends out a message when the boys are discovered missing. Prepare a news report to tell of the event.

❑ Free choice—Prepare a proposal form and submit your idea to the teacher for approval.

---

### 8 Points

❑ Hold Your Nose Billy was very proud of the fact that people sang a song about him. Create a song about Jemmy and Prince Brat telling of their adventures and perform it for the class.

❑ As the story progresses, the reader can really begin to see why Prince Brat acts the way he does. Write three journal entries from the Prince's point of view describing his feeling towards some of the major events that occurred in the book. Try to pick one near the beginning of the story, one when they are in the forest, and one at the end of the story.

# The Whipping Boy Cube

Jemmy proved his intelligence many times throughout this novel. Find six quotes from the novel that show his intelligence and create a cube of examples. Use this pattern or create your own cube.

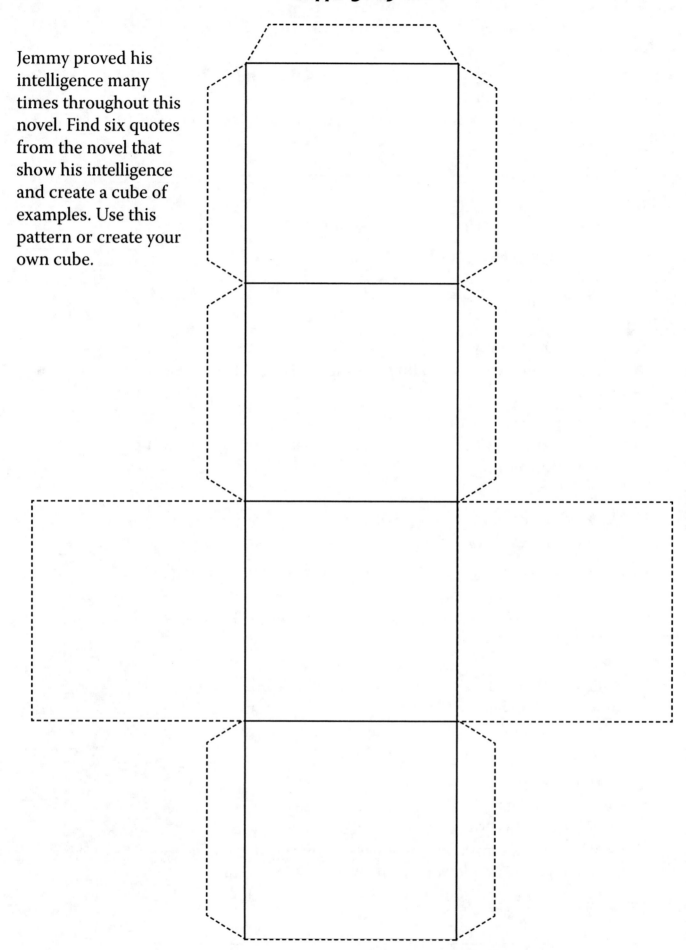

# How to Eat Fried Worms

## 2-5-8 Menu

In *How to Eat Fried Worms*, four boys are talking about the grand deeds that they would or would not do for money. During this discussion, Billy says that he would eat worms; in fact, for $50, he would eat 15 worms. His friends immediately decide this would be a great bet and set the terms. He will have 15 days to eat 15 worms. They can be prepared anyway he would like, and he must eat them in the presence of another boy in the group. The culinary adventures continue as Billy eats his daily worms, and as he gets closer to his goal, the other boys try to trick him into not completing the bet.

### Reading Objectives Covered Through This Menu and These Activities

- Students will show comprehension by retelling or acting out events in the story.
- Students will show comprehension by summarizing the story.
- Students will recognize story problems or plot.
- Students will represent textual information by using story maps.
- Students will make and explain inferences made from the story.
- Students will draw conclusions and make predictions on what is read in the story.

### Writing Objectives Covered Through This Menu and These Activities

- Students will write to express, develop, reflect, or problem solve.
- Students will write to inform, explain, describe, or narrate.
- Students will write to entertain.
- Students will use vivid language.

### Materials Needed by Students for Completion

- *How to Eat Fried Worms* by Thomas Rockwell
- Video camera (for news report)
- Microsoft PowerPoint or other slideshow software
- Cube template
- Story map of teacher's choice

### Time Frame

- 1–2 weeks—Students are given the menu as the unit is started, and the teacher discusses all of the product options on the menu. As the different options are discussed, students will choose products that add to a total of 10 points. As the lessons progress through the week, the teacher and students refer back to the options associated with the content being taught.

- 1–2 days—The teacher chooses an activity from the menu to use with the entire class.

## Suggested Forms
- All-purpose rubric
- Student-taught lesson rubric

## *How to Eat Fried Worms*

**Directions:** Choose two activities from the menu below. The activities must total 10 points. Place a checkmark next to each box to show which activities you will complete. All activities must be completed by _____.

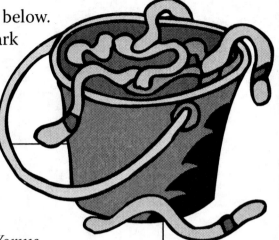

---

### 2 Points

❒ Complete a story map for *How to Eat Fried Worms*.

❒ Complete the story cube for *How to Eat Fried Worms*.

---

### 5 Points

❒ In this story, the boys tried to find the biggest worms they could so Billy wouldn't win the bet. Research different types of worms and create an informational pamphlet on the different types and sizes.

❒ Create a new book cover for *How to Eat Fried Worms*.

❒ Joe and Alan wrote a letter to Billy's mother trying to convince her that eating worms was medically bad for him. Pretend you are Joe and Alan and create another letter to send to Billy's father reinforcing this same idea, as well as other reasons why you think he shouldn't eat the worms.

❒ Create a news report about the worm-eating bet and its final outcome.

---

### 8 Points

❒ Although this book does have a short epilogue, perhaps Billy's eating adventures are not over. Write your own sequel that tells of the boys' next adventure.

❒ Of all the recipes the boys and Billy's mom created, which did you think was the best? Why do you think this? Do your own research by looking through several cookbooks and develop three tasty worm recipes of your own. Record the recipes, including ingredients and preparation steps.

---

# How to Eat Fried Worms Cube

Complete this cube about the book *How to Eat Fried Worms.* Use this pattern or create your own cube.

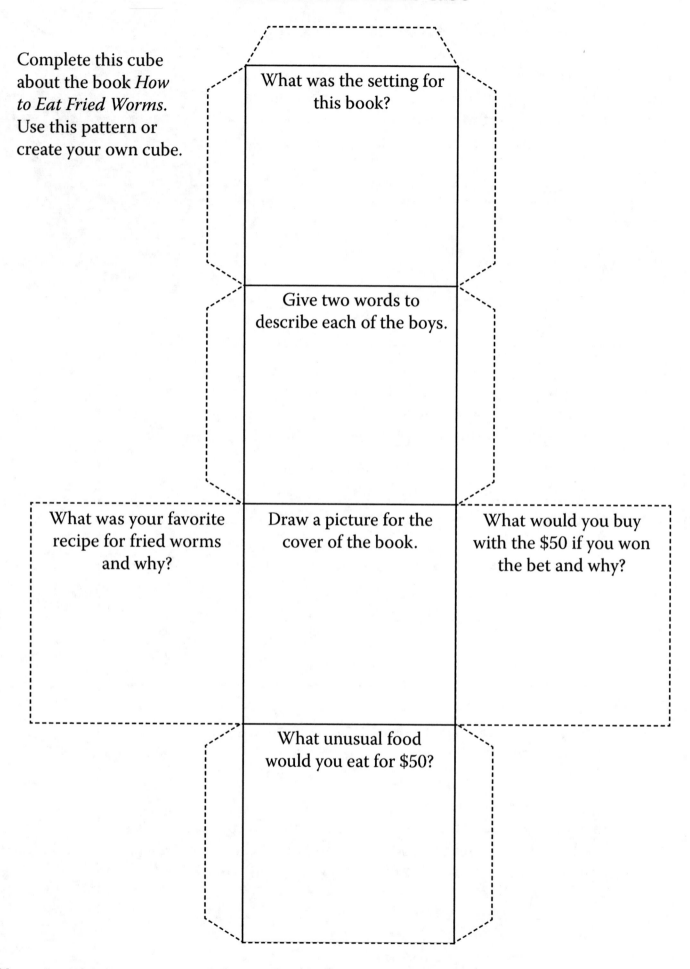

What was the setting for this book?

Give two words to describe each of the boys.

What was your favorite recipe for fried worms and why?

Draw a picture for the cover of the book.

What would you buy with the $50 if you won the bet and why?

What unusual food would you eat for $50?

## *Snow Treasure*

## Tic-Tac-Toe Menu

When the Nazis invade Hungary, a plan is made to smuggle the gold out of the country so the Nazis will not find it. *Snow Treasure* describes how the gold is first moved to a cave and then it must be transported a long distance across the snow to a waiting hidden ship. The adults in the town come up with the perfect plan: The children will move the gold a few bars at a time as they sled right under the noses of the Nazis. It isn't as easy as it seems, or is it?

### Reading Objectives Covered Through This Menu and These Activities
- Students will show comprehension by retelling or acting out events in the story.
- Students will show comprehension by summarizing the story.
- Students will analyze characters, their relationships, and their importance in the story.
- Students will recognize story problems or plot.
- Students will make and explain inferences made from the story.
- Students will draw conclusions and make predictions on what is read in the story.

### Writing Objectives Covered Through This Menu and These Activities
- Students will write to express, develop, reflect, or problem solve.
- Students will write to inform, explain, describe, or narrate.
- Students will write to entertain.
- Students will exhibit voice in their writing.

### Materials Needed by Students for Completion
- *Snow Treasure* by Marie McSwigan
- Magazines (for collage)
- Video camera (for news report)
- Microsoft PowerPoint or other slideshow software

### Time Frame
- 2 weeks—Students are given the menu as the unit is started. As the teacher presents lessons throughout the week, he or she should refer back to the options associated with that content. The teacher will go over all of the options for that content and have students place

checkmarks in the boxes that represent the activities they are most interested in completing. As teaching continues during the 2 weeks, activities chosen and completed should make a column or a row.

- 1 week—At the start of the unit, the teacher chooses the three activities he or she feels are most valuable for the students. Stations can be set up in the classroom. These three activities are available for student choice throughout the week, as regular instruction takes place.
- 1–2 days—The teacher chooses an activity from the menu to use with the entire class.

## Suggested Forms

- All-purpose rubric
- Proposal forms

Name:_____

## *Snow Treasure*

| ☐ Create a PowerPoint Presentation | ☐ Interview a Character | ☐ Then What? |
|---|---|---|
| Countries often keep gold as a reserve of their country's wealth. Research how the United States keeps its gold safe. Prepare a PowerPoint presentation to share this information. | Jan had many experiences with the Nazis and Norwegians. Pretend you are a newspaper writer and create an interview for him about his experiences. | Write a story that tells about Peter's life after *Snow Treasure* has ended. What other adventures did he experience, and how has his life changed? |
| ☐ Design a Book Cover | ☐ Free Choice | ☐ They Did What? |
| After reading *Snow Treasure*, design your own book cover for this novel. | (Fill out your proposal form before beginning the free choice!) | Imagine that you are a reporter in the United States who has just heard about the gold in Hungary and how it was smuggled out by children. Present a news report about the deed. |
| ☐ Present a Play | ☐ Write a Letter | ☐ Make a Collage |
| Choose one of the most dramatic scenes in the book and write a play for that scene. With the help of a few of your classmates, present the play. | At the end of the story, Peter finds himself embarking on another adventure. Write a letter from Peter to his mother explaining what has happened and his feelings about the changes that have occurred. | Think about all the characteristics a child would have to possess to complete the task of smuggling gold out of the country. Create a collage of words or pictures to show these qualities. |

Check the boxes you plan to complete. They should form a tic-tac-toe across or down. All products are due by: _____.

# *Maniac Magee*

## List Menu

In *Maniac Magee*, Jeffrey Magee's parents die, and he goes to live with his aunt and uncle. This is not a happy situation, so he runs away. Jeffrey finds himself in a town called Two Mills. Although Two Mills is a segregated town, Jeffrey becomes a bridge across these boundaries as he performs acts of heroism earning him the nickname "Maniac Magee" and legendary status.

### *Reading Objectives Covered Through This Menu and These Activities*
*   Students will show comprehension by retelling or acting out events in the story.
*   Students will show comprehension by summarizing the story.
*   Students will analyze characters, their relationships, and their importance in the story.
*   Students will represent textual information by using story maps.
*   Students will make and explain inferences made from the story.

### *Writing Objectives Covered Through This Menu and These Activities*
*   Students will support their responses with textual evidence.
*   Students will write to inform, explain, describe, or narrate.

### *Materials Needed by Students for Completion*
*   *Maniac Magee* by Jerry Spinelli
*   Materials for board games (e.g., folders, colored cards, etc.)
*   Microsoft PowerPoint or other slideshow software
*   Cube template
*   Story map of teacher's choice

### *Time Frame*
*   1–2 weeks—Students are given the menu as the unit is started and the guidelines and point expectations are discussed. Because this menu covers one topic in depth, the teacher will go over all of the options on the menu and have students place checkmarks in the boxes next to the activities they are most interested in completing. Once the students have placed checkmarks next to the activities they are interested in, teachers will set aside a few moments to sign the agreement

at the bottom of the page with each student. As instruction continues, activities are completed by students and submitted for grading.

- 1–2 days—The teacher chooses an activity from an objective to use with the entire class during that lesson time.

## *Suggested Forms*

- All-purpose rubric
- Proposal form for point-based projects

Name:_____

# *Maniac Magee* Challenge Investigation

*Guidelines:*
1. You may complete as many of the activities listed as you would like within the time period given.
2. You may choose any combination of activities.
3. Your goal is 100 points. You may earn up to _____ points in extra credit.
4. You may be as creative as you like within the guidelines listed below.
5. You must show your plan to your teacher by _____.
6. Activities may be turned in at any time during the working time period. They will be graded and recorded on this sheet as you continue to work, so keep it safe!

| Plan to Do | Activity to Complete | Point Value | Date Completed | Points Earned |
|---|---|---|---|---|
| | Create your own jump rope rhyme about the famous Maniac Magee. Be prepared to perform it outside for your classmates. | 30 | | |
| | Research the life of Jerry Spinelli. Prepare a PowerPoint presentation about him and other books he has written. | 20 | | |
| | Make a Venn diagram to compare and contrast your home and family with the McNabb's home and family. | 20 | | |
| | Write a newspaper article about the now-famous Jeffrey Magee and all of his accomplishments. | 25 | | |
| | Choose one scene from *Maniac Magee* and perform it for your classmates. | 30 | | |
| | Maniac is always running, but sometimes there are different reasons for his running. Develop an interview where you ask Maniac about his running. Provide his answers with support from the text. | 30 | | |
| | Create a thank-you greeting card for Maniac to give to Amanda for lending him one of her books. | 25 | | |
| | Design a board game about the town of Two Mills. Your players should encounter similar adventures as outlined in the book. | 25 | | |
| | Complete a story map for *Maniac Magee*. | 10 | | |
| | Write a journal entry to document the first day Maniac comes to Two Mills and all of his adventures. | 25 | | |
| | It was very important to Maniac that he has an address. Construct a project cube that has examples from the text to support this statement. | 30 | | |
| | Free choice: Must be outlined on a proposal form and approved before beginning work. | Up to 30 | | |
| | **Total number of points you are planning to earn.** | | **Total points earned** | |

I am planning to complete _____ activities that could earn up to a total of _____ points.

Teacher's initials _____ Student's signature _____

# *Maniac Magee* Cube

It was very important to Maniac that he has an address. Construct a project cube that has examples from the text to support this statement. Use this pattern or create your own cube.

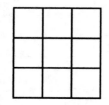

# *James and the Giant Peach*

## Tic-Tac-Toe Menu

In *James and the Giant Peach*, James is living with his abusive aunts and his life seems to get worse each day. One day, he is given some green seeds that were supposed to be magical. He accidentally drops the seeds, which grow into a large peach tree. When he examines one of the peaches, he finds a door and enters. Here he meets some interesting characters and his adventures begin to lead him to a better life.

### Reading Objectives Covered Through This Menu and These Activities

- Students will analyze characters, their relationships, and their importance in the story.
- Students will recognize story problems or plot.
- Students will make and explain inferences made from the story.
- Students will draw conclusions and make predictions on what is read in the story.

### Writing Objectives Covered Through This Menu and These Activities

- Students will write to inform, explain, describe, or narrate.
- Students will write to entertain.
- Students will exhibit voice in their writing.
- Students will use vivid language.

### Materials Needed by Students for Completion

- *James and the Giant Peach* by Roald Dahl
- Materials for student-created models (e.g., peach)
- Blank index cards (for trading cards)

### Special Notes on the Use of this Menu

This menu gives students the option of designing an experiment to test the buoyancy of different fruits. Students will not need any complex equipment to complete this. They should prepare a lab report to show how the experiment will be conducted. If you do not teach science, check with your science teacher so this activity can reinforce his or her expectations for a lab report. The demonstration for the class should not take longer than 2–3 minutes.

## Time Frame

- 2 weeks—Students are given the menu as the unit is started and the guidelines and point expectations are discussed. As lessons are taught throughout the unit, students and the teacher can refer back to the options associated with that topic. The teacher will go over all of the options for the topic being covered and have students place checkmarks in the boxes next to the activities they are most interested in completing. As teaching continues during next 2 weeks, activities chosen and completed should make a column or row.
- 1 week—At the start of the unit, the teacher chooses the three activities he or she feels are most valuable for the students. Stations can be set up in the classroom. These three activities are available for student choice throughout the week, as regular instruction takes place.
- 1–2 days—The teacher chooses an activity from the menu to use with the entire class.

## Suggested Forms

- All-purpose rubric
- Proposal forms

Name:_____

## *James and the Giant Peach*

| | | |
|---|---|---|
| ☐ *Write an Article*<br>James had quite a wild ride in his peach. Write a newspaper article that could have reported his landing on the Empire State Building. | ☐ *Design an Experiment*<br>The peach James traveled in floated across the ocean. Do peaches really float? Develop an experiment to test the buoyancy of a peach, as well as 3–4 other popular fruits. Share your results with your class. | ☐ *Make a Drawing*<br>James found some true friends through his adventures in this story. Make a drawing of a true friend. The drawing must include at least seven characteristics you think a true friend should have. |
| ☐ *Write a Story*<br>Although James traveled in a peach, how might his trip have been different if he had traveled in a different type of fruit (or vegetable)? Write a story that tells of his adventures in another fruit or vegetable of your choice. | ☐ **Free Choice**<br>(Fill out your proposal form before beginning the free choice!) | ☐ *Write a Letter*<br>Now that James has settled happily in New York, write a letter from James to his aunts that were left behind telling of his new life. |
| ☐ *Create a Model*<br>Create a model of the inside of James' peach based on what you read in the story. | ☐ *Make Trading Cards*<br>There were a lot of interesting and important characters in this story. Make a set of trading cards with one card for each character. Include their pictures and important facts about their personalities. | ☐ *Design a Travel Brochure*<br>Perhaps James should start a Travel by Peach travel agency. Create a brochure that would outline trips customers could take via a peach. |

Check the boxes you plan to complete. They should form a tic-tac-toe across or down. All products are due by: _____.

# *From Anna*

# List Menu

*From Anna* is the story of Anna, the youngest in a large German family, who is always being picked on by her brothers and sisters. She is even given the nickname "Awkward Anna" because of her clumsiness, and her inability to read and write well. When her uncle dies, her father decides to move the family from Germany to Canada to run his brother's store. This is a huge change for Anna, who blatantly refuses to learn English when they arrive. During a visit to the doctor, it is quickly discovered that Anna has serious problems with her eyesight and needs glasses. These glasses open up a whole new world for Anna. Her life changes after that day. Will the rest of the family see what she does now?

## *Reading Objectives Covered Through This Menu and These Activities*

- Students will show comprehension by summarizing the story.
- Students will analyze characters, their relationships, and their importance in the story.
- Students will represent textual information by using story maps.
- Students will make and explain inferences made from the story.
- Students will draw conclusions and make predictions on what is read in the story.

## *Writing Objectives Covered Through This Menu and These Activities*

- Students will support their responses with textual evidence.
- Students will write to express, develop, reflect, or problem solve.
- Students will write to inform, explain, describe, or narrate.
- Students will write to entertain.
- Students will exhibit voice in their writing.

## *Materials Needed by Students for Completion*

- *From Anna* by Jean Little
- *A Child's Garden of Verses* by Robert Louis Stevenson
- Poster board or large white paper
- Story map of teacher's choice
- Materials for basket making (if you allow this activity)
- Magazines (for collage)

*Time Frame*

- 1–2 weeks—Students are given the menu as the unit is started and the guidelines and point expectations are discussed. Because this menu covers one topic in depth, the teacher will go over all of the options on the menu and have students place checkmarks in the boxes next to the activities they are most interested in completing. Once the students have placed checkmarks next to the activities they are interested in, teachers will set aside a few moments to sign the agreement at the bottom of the page with each student. As instruction continues, activities are completed by students and submitted for grading.
- 1–2 days—The teacher chooses an activity from an objective to use with the entire class during that lesson time.

*Suggested Forms*

- All-purpose rubric
- Proposal form for point-based projects

Name:_____

# *From Anna* Challenge Investigation

## Guidelines:

1. You may complete as many of the activities listed as you would like within the time period given.
2. You may choose any combination of activities.
3. Your goal is 100 points. You may earn up to _____ points in extra credit.
4. You may be as creative as you like within the guidelines listed below.
5. You must show your plan to your teacher by _____.
6. Activities may be turned in at any time during the working time period. They will be graded and recorded on this sheet as you continue to work, so keep it safe!

| Plan to Do | Activity to Complete | Point Value | Date Completed | Points Earned |
|---|---|---|---|---|
| | Create a German picture dictionary for words you use on a daily basis. | 20 | | |
| | Glasses opened a new world for Anna. Research how eyeglasses help people see better and make a poster about your findings. | 20 | | |
| | Complete a story map for *From Anna*. | 15 | | |
| | Anna was always very upset with herself; create a motivational collage of her good qualities. | 25 | | |
| | When money was tight at Christmas, the children came up a good solution. What kinds of ideas would you come up with to solve the problem? Write an instruction sheet for how you would make your item. | 25 | | |
| | The gift that Anna gave her parents was meaningful in many different ways. Make a window pane with all the various meanings in the different panes. | 30 | | |
| | Anna loved to sing songs because of the meanings of the words. Choose one of your favorite songs that you enjoy. Write down the words, explain why you find the words meaningful, and perform the song for your teacher. | 30 | | |
| | A wonderful poem was written about Ben for a gift. Choose someone special to you and write a similar poem for them. Give them the poem as a gift. | 30 | | |
| | Create a Venn diagram to compare and contrast Germany and Canada. | 20 | | |
| | Read *A Child's Garden of Verses*. Choose the poem that has the most meaning for you. Share your poem with the class and why you chose that one. | 30 | | |
| | Research how to make baskets. Using reeds, make your own basket. | 30 | | |
| | Free choice: Must be outlined on a proposal form and approved before beginning work. | Up to 30 | | |
| | **Total number of points you are planning to earn.** | | **Total points earned** | |

I am planning to complete _____ activities that could earn up to a total of _____ points.

Teacher's initials _____ Student's signature _____

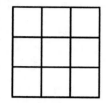

# *Tuck Everlasting*

# Tic-Tac-Toe Menu

In *Tuck Everlasting*, Winnie is an overprotected young lady who befriends the Tuck family. Winnie soon discovers that the Tucks have an unique family secret. They have a special spring on the property that gives eternal life; the drinker will never age or die. The Tucks have developed ways to deal with this situation, but when a man comes to try and take the water to sell, Mae Tuck kills the man. Mae cannot die, nor will she age, and if put in jail the Tucks' secret will be discovered. What can be done?

### *Reading Objectives Covered Through This Menu and These Activities*
- Students will show comprehension by retelling or acting out events in the story.
- Students will recognize story problems or plot.
- Students will make and explain inferences made from the story.
- Students will draw conclusions and make predictions on what is read in the story.

### *Writing Objectives Covered Through This Menu and These Activities*
- Students will support their responses with textual evidence.
- Students will write to inform, explain, describe, or narrate.
- Students will write to entertain.

### *Materials Needed by Students for Completion*
- *Tuck Everlasting* by Natalie Babbitt
- Poster board or large white paper
- Video camera (for commercial)
- Cube template

### *Time Frame*
- 2 weeks—Students are given the menu as the unit is started and the guidelines and point expectations are discussed. As lessons are taught throughout the unit, students and the teacher can refer back to the options associated with that topic. The teacher will go over all of the options for the topic being covered and have students place checkmarks in the boxes next to the activities they are most interested in completing. As teaching continues during next 2 weeks, activities chosen and completed should make a column or a row.

- 1 week—At the start of the unit, the teacher chooses the three activities he or she feels are most valuable for the students. Stations can be set up in the classroom. These three activities are available for student choice throughout the week, as regular instruction takes place.
- 1–2 days—The teacher chooses an activity from the menu to use with the entire class.

### Suggested Forms

- All-purpose rubric
- Proposal Forms

## Tuck Everlasting

| | | |
|---|---|---|
| ☐ *Write a Story*<br><br>Although the author provides an epilogue to the novel, create your own version of what may have happened after the story ended. | ☐ *Design a Book Cover*<br><br>After reading *Tuck Everlasting*, design your own book cover for the novel. | ☐ *Prepare a Poster*<br><br>Throughout history, people have searched for the fountain of youth. Research one of these people and prepare a poster about where his or her searches led that person. |
| ☐ *Write a Play*<br><br>Choose the most important part of the book in your opinion and rewrite it as a play. With the help of your classmates, perform this scene for your classmates. | ☐ *Free Choice*<br><br>(Fill out your proposal form before beginning the free choice!) | ☐ *Create a Venn Diagram*<br><br>Winnie found a lot of differences between her family and the Tucks. Create a Venn diagram to compare and contrast the two families. |
| ☐ *Create a Commercial*<br><br>The water from the spring could be very valuable. If the man in the yellow suit had been able to obtain the spring water, create a commercial he may have used to sell the water. | ☐ *Write a Letter*<br><br>Winnie made her decision about drinking from the spring. Do you think it was the right decision? Write a letter to Winnie explaining whether you agree or disagree with her actions. | ☐ *Complete a Cube*<br><br>*Tuck Everlasting* has many different facets. Complete the Tuck cube for this novel. |

Check the boxes you plan to complete. They should form a tic-tac-toe across or down. All products are due by: _____.

# *Tuck Everlasting* Cube

Complete the cube for *Tuck Everlasting*. Respond to the questions on each side to analyze this novel in depth. Use this pattern or create your own cube.

What was the problem faced in this novel?

Do you think there really is a fountain of youth? Explain.

Which character is most like you? Why?

Describe the setting of this novel.

What would be another good name for this novel? Why?

Which character was most important to this story? Why?

# *The Cay*

# List Menu

*The Cay* is a book about Phillip and his mother, who are living on the island of Curacao when World War II begins. She decides it would be safer for them to travel back to Virginia but when their ship sinks, Phillip finds himself in a challenging situation. The accident leaves him blind and alone on a small island with a Black man named Timothy and a cat. He has many problems to overcome, including his blindness, his prejudice, and learning to survive on the small island.

### *Reading Objectives Covered Through This Menu and These Activities*
- Students will represent textual information by using story maps.
- Students will make and explain inferences made from the story.
- Students will draw conclusions and make predictions on what is read in the story.
- Students will distinguish fact from opinion.

### *Writing Objectives Covered Through This Menu and These Activities*
- Students will write to express, develop, reflect, or problem solve.
- Students will write to inform, explain, describe, or narrate.
- Students will exhibit voice in their writing.

### *Materials Needed by Students for Completion*
- *The Cay* by Theodore Taylor
- Materials for board games (e.g., folders, colored cards, etc.)
- Materials for student-created models
- Microsoft PowerPoint or other slideshow software
- Story map of teacher's choice
- Scrapbooking materials

### *Time Frame*
- 1–2 weeks—Students are given the menu as the unit is started and the guidelines and point expectations are discussed. Because this menu covers one topic in depth, the teacher will go over all of the options on the menu and have students place checkmarks in the boxes next to the activities they are most interested in completing. Once the students have placed checkmarks next to the activities they are interested in, teachers will set aside a few moments to sign the agreement

at the bottom of the page with each student. As instruction continues, activities are completed by students and submitted for grading.

- 1–2 days—The teacher chooses an activity from an objective to use with the entire class during that lesson time.

## Suggested Forms

- All-purpose rubric
- Proposal form for point-based projects

Name:_____

# *The Cay* Challenge Investigation

## Guidelines:

1. You may complete as many of the activities listed as you would like within the time period given.
2. You may choose any combination of activities.
3. Your goal is 100 points. You may earn up to _____ points in extra credit.
4. You may be as creative as you like within the guidelines listed below.
5. You must show your plan to your teacher by _____.
6. Activities may be turned in at any time during the working time period. They will be graded and recorded on this sheet as you continue to work, so keep it safe!

| Plan to Do | Activity to Complete | Point Value | Date Completed | Points Earned |
|---|---|---|---|---|
| | Make a model of the island where Timothy and Phillip spent their time. | 20 | | |
| | Prepare a PowerPoint presentation on the West Indies. | 20 | | |
| | Complete a story map for *The Cay*. | 15 | | |
| | The chapters in this book are not titled. Write your own title for each chapter in a table of contents and explain why you chose each title. | 25 | | |
| | Create a scrapbook documenting Phillip's stay on the island. | 25 | | |
| | Write a news report about Phillip's rescue. | 25 | | |
| | Create a board game based on *The Cay*. | 25 | | |
| | Create a T-chart to show at least five facts found in the story and five examples of fiction. | 15 | | |
| | The Caribbean is known for a special type of music. Research the history of this music and write your own song about *The Cay* that could be accompanied by this musical style. | 30 | | |
| | Write three journal entries from Phillip's point of view: one when he first arrived on the cay, one right after the change with Timothy, and one after he was reunited with his family. | 30 | | |
| | If you were taking a long voyage as Phillip was, what would you want to take with you in case of shipwreck? Create your own survival kit. | 25 | | |
| | Although Timothy did not have a grave marker, write the epitaph that Phillip may have left if he had the ability to do so. | 25 | | |
| | There are many memorable passages in this book. Choose one of your favorite quotes and design a motivational poster based on your quote. | 30 | | |
| | Free choice: Must be outlined on a proposal form and approved before beginning work. | Up to 30 | | |
| | **Total number of points you are planning to earn.** | | **Total points earned** | |

I am planning to complete _____ activities that could earn up to a total of _____ points.

Teacher's initials _____ Student's signature _____

# CHAPTER 7

# Mechanics

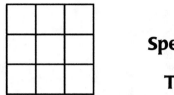

# Spelling/Vocabulary I

# Tic-Tac-Toe Menu

*Reading Objectives Covered Through This Menu and These Activities*
- Students will use resources and references to build word meanings.
- Students will interpret figurative language and multiple meaning words.

*Writing Objectives Covered Through This Menu and These Activities*
- Students will write to express, develop, reflect, or problem solve.
- Students will write to inform, explain, describe, or narrate.

*Materials Needed by Students for Completion*
- Graph paper or Internet access (for crossword puzzle)
- Blank index cards (for concentration game)
- Cube template

*Special Notes on the Use of this Menu*
This menu can be used for either spelling or vocabulary words, with a focus on the use of these words and their definitions. All activities will refer to the target words as weekly words. The teacher will choose whether these are spelling or vocabulary words.

*Time Frame*
- 1 week—
    *Individual Work*—Students are given the menu at the beginning of the week with their weekly words. The teacher will go over all of the options for using the words and have students place checks in the boxes that represent the activities they are most interested in completing. As the week continues, activities chosen and completed should make a column or a row.
    *Centers*—This menu (or chosen activities from the menu) can also be placed at centers and students can choose what they would like to complete for the week. If the teacher uses one choice, as well as the free choice each week, this could be a 8-week rotation for a spelling center.
- 1–2 days—The teacher chooses an activity from the menu to use with the entire class.

*Suggested Forms*
- All-purpose rubric
- Proposal forms

# Spelling/Vocabulary I

| | | |
|---|---|---|
| ☐ *Compose a Letter*<br>Write a letter to your parents or one of your classmates. Use at least half of your weekly words in your letter and make sure they are used correctly. | ☐ *Make an Acrostic*<br>Make an acrostic for two of your weekly words. The words you choose for each letter should be related to the word written downward. | ☐ *Design Gestures*<br>Choose four of your weekly words that you have trouble remembering. Develop some hand motions to help you remember them and share them with your classmates. |
| ☐ *Create a Cube*<br>Complete a spelling cube for six of your weekly words. | ☐ **Free Choice**<br>(Fill out your proposal form before beginning the free choice!) | ☐ *Complete Concentration*<br>Create a set of concentration cards for your weekly words. On one set of cards, use the word. The other set can have pictures or a written definition for each. |
| ☐ *Create a Crossword Puzzle*<br>Using all of your weekly words, create a crossword puzzle. You can be creative on the clues that you use. Do not always use the definition for the clue! | ☐ *Make Your Own Dictionary*<br>Make a rhyming dictionary for your weekly words. Record each word with at least four words that rhyme with that word. | ☐ *Write a Story*<br>Using all of your weekly words, write a story about the adventures of Word-O, a crazy superhero. |

Check the boxes you plan to complete. They should form a tic-tac-toe across or down. All products are due by: _____.

# Weekly Word Cube

Each side of this cube should have one of your weekly words, a definition for that word, and a picture that describes the word. Use this pattern or create your own cube.

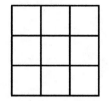

# Spelling/Vocabulary II—Word Building

## Tic-Tac-Toe Menu

*Reading Objectives Covered Through This Menu and These Activities*
- Students will use resources and references to build word meanings.
- Students will interpret figurative language and multiple meaning words.

*Writing Objectives Covered Through This Menu and These Activities*
- Students will write to inform, explain, describe, or narrate.

*Materials Needed by Students for Completion*
- Blank index cards (for flip card game)
- Ruler (for comic strip)

*Special Notes on the Use of this Menu*
This menu can be used for either spelling or vocabulary words, with a focus on the dissection of the words and the use of prefixes and suffixes to build new words. All activities will refer to the target words as weekly words. The teacher will choose whether these are spelling or vocabulary words.

*Time Frame*
- 1 week—
    *Individual Work*—Students are given the menu at the beginning of the week with their weekly words. The teacher will go over all of the options for using the words and have students place checks in the boxes that represent the activities they are most interested in completing. As the week continues, activities chosen and completed should make a column or a row.
    *Centers*—This menu (or chosen activities from the menu) can also be placed at centers and students can choose what they would like to complete for the week. If the teacher uses one choice, as well as the free choice each week, this could be a 8-week rotation for a spelling center.
- 1–2 days—The teacher chooses an activity from the menu to use with the entire class.

*Suggested Forms*
- All-purpose rubric
- Proposal forms

# Spelling/Vocabulary II—Word Building Menu

| | | |
|---|---|---|
| ☐ **Create a Categorization Chart**<br><br>Using all of your words for this week, categorize them into nouns, verbs, adjectives, and pronouns. | ☐ **Create a Comic Strip**<br><br>Using your creativity, create a comic strip that uses at least four of your words for this week. | ☐ **Develop a Game**<br><br>When you add prefixes and suffixes to words, you change their meaning. Create a flip card game that could add three prefixes and suffixes to your words. Record the new words you have created and their definitions. |
| ☐ **Identify New Words**<br><br>Using all of your words for this week, identify new words by adding prefixes and suffixes. Record the new words you have created and their definitions. | ☐ **Free Choice**<br><br>(Fill out your proposal form before beginning the free choice!) | ☐ **Dissect a Word**<br><br>Choose two of your weekly words. Looking at all of the letters, record all of the shorter words that could be made with these letters. |
| ☐ **Write a Song**<br><br>Write a song or rap using at least half of your weekly words. Be prepared to share it with your class. | ☐ **Calculate a Word's Value**<br><br>Using the word calculator below, calculate the value of three of your weekly words. Calculate the change after adding a prefix or suffix. Are there any words that could lose value because of spelling changes? | ☐ **Changing Words**<br><br>Using half of your weekly words, make a list that changes their parts of speech. Defend the change you made. For example, you could change *write* (verb) into *written* (adjective). |

Check the boxes you plan to complete. They should form a tic-tac-toe across or down. All products are due by: _____.

## Word Calculator

| A | B | C | D | E | F | G | H | I | J | K | L | M |
|---|---|---|---|---|---|---|---|---|---|---|---|---|
| 4¢ | 5¢ | 2¢ | 3¢ | 4¢ | 6¢ | 9¢ | 1¢ | 7¢ | 10¢ | 8¢ | 2¢ | 5¢ |

| N | O | P | Q | R | S | T | U | V | W | X | Y | Z |
|---|---|---|---|---|---|---|---|---|---|---|---|---|
| 6¢ | 9¢ | 5¢ | 8¢ | 4¢ | 12¢ | 2¢ | 5¢ | 14¢ | 3¢ | 13¢ | 15¢ | 40¢ |

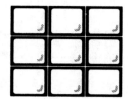

# Word Play

# Game Show Menu

## Reading Objectives Covered Through This Menu and These Activities
- Students will use resources and references to build word meanings.
- Students will interpret figurative language and multiple meaning words.

## Writing Objectives Covered Through This Menu and These Activities
- Students will write to inform, explain, describe, or narrate.
- Students will write to entertain.
- Students will exhibit voice in their writing.
- Students will use vivid language.

## Materials Needed by Students for Completion
- Poster board or large white paper
- Graph paper or Internet access (for crossword puzzle)
- Microsoft PowerPoint or other slideshow software
- Blank index cards (for concentration card game)

## Special Notes on the Use of this Menu
One of the activities for this menu has students design their own children's book based on antonyms. A wonderful example is *Is It Dark? Is It Light?* by Mary Lankford.

## Time Frame
- 1–3 weeks—This menu can be taught as a separate unit, but it works best when used in conjunction with weekly words or a novel study. The menu can be given to students with the expectation that by the end of a grading period, a student would have completed 90 points in the four areas.
- 1–2 days—The teacher chooses an activity from an objective to use with the entire class during that lesson time or at a center.

## Suggested Forms
- All-purpose rubric
- Proposal form for point-based projects

## Guidelines for Word Play Game Show Menu

- You must choose at least one activity from each topic area.
- You may not do more than two activities in any one topic area for credit. (You are, of course, welcome to do more than two for your own investigation.)
- Grading will be ongoing, so turn in products as you complete them.
- All free-choice proposals must be turned in and approved *prior* to working on that free choice.
- You must earn 90 points for a 100%. You may earn extra credit up to _____ points.
- You must show your teacher your plan for completion by: _____.

# Word Play

| Homophones | Synonyms | Antonyms | Multiple Meaning Words | Points for Each Level |
|---|---|---|---|---|
| ☐ Complete the homophone brainstorming activity. (10 pts.) | ☐ Make a set of concentration cards for pairs of at least 10 synonyms. (10 pts.) | ☐ Make a window pane of antonyms with at least 10 sets of words. (10 pts.) | ☐ Using a dictionary, look up the word *run*. Make a poster showing pictures for at least half of the definitions for run. (15 pts.) | 10–15 points |
| ☐ Design a game for your classmates that tests their knowledge of homophones. (20 pts.) | ☐ Create two word webs: one for the word *good*, and one for the word *nice*. Brainstorm synonyms for these words that could be used in your writing instead. (20 pts.) | ☐ Design a worksheet for a student that tests their knowledge of antonyms. (20 pts.) | ☐ Design a crossword puzzle with at least five multiple meaning words. (20 pts.) | 20–25 points |
| ☐ Create a poem using at least 10 different sets of homophones. (30 pts.) | ☐ Write a funny yet descriptive story about a day in the life of a bug. Warning: You cannot use any of the words on the Banned List Chart at the bottom of this page. (30 pts.) | ☐ Design your own children's 20-questions book based on antonyms. (30 pts.) | ☐ Create a PowerPoint quiz that uses multiple meaning words and tests the reader's ability to identify their meanings. (30 pts.) | 30 points |
| ☐ **Free Choice** (prior approval) **(25–50 pts.)** | ☐ **Free Choice** (prior approval) **(25–50 pts.)** | ☐ **Free Choice** (prior approval) **(25–50 pts.)** | ☐ **Free Choice** (prior approval) **(25–50 pts.)** | 25–50 points |
| **Total:** | **Total:** | **Total:** | **Total:** | **Total Grade:** |

### Banned List of Words

| | | | | |
|---|---|---|---|---|
| good | bad | fun | like | said | hot |
| cold | happy | sad | mad | go | blue |

# Brainstorming Homophones

As you know, homophones are words that sound the same but have different spellings and meanings.

## The Basics

Listed below is one word in a homophone pair. Write the other word in the pair.

| | |
|---|---|
| Allowed | Packed |
| Beach | Pale |
| Days | Rain |
| Great | Road |
| Lane | Seen |
| Leek | Waste |

## The Challenge

Your challenge is to write three sentences using a pair of homophones from the table above in the same sentence.

Example: I heard the loud, thundering herd of elephants.
Write your own sentences below.

1. _____

_____

2. _____

_____

3. _____

_____

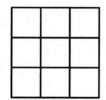

# Reference Materials

# Tic-Tac-Toe Menu

## *Reading Objectives Covered Through This Menu and These Activities*
- Students will use resources and references to build word meanings.

## *Writing Objectives Covered Through This Menu and These Activities*
- Students will write to express, develop, reflect, or problem solve.
- Students will write to inform, explain, describe, or narrate.
- Students will write to entertain.
- Students will exhibit voice in their writing.

## *Materials Needed by Students for Completion*
- Poster board or large white paper
- Coat hangers (mobile)
- Index cards (mobile)
- String (mobile)
- Blank index cards (recipe cards)

## *Time Frame*
- 2 weeks—Students are given the menu as the unit is started and the guidelines and point expectations are discussed. As lessons are taught throughout the unit, students and the teacher can refer back to the options associated with that topic. The teacher will go over all of the options for the topic being covered and have students place check-marks in the boxes next to the activities they are most interested in completing. As teaching continues during next 2 weeks, activities chosen and completed should make a column or row.
- 1 week—At the start of the unit, the teacher chooses the three activities he or she feels are most valuable for the students. Stations can be set up in the classroom. These three activities are available for student choice throughout the week, as regular instruction takes place.
- 1–2 days—The teacher chooses an activity from the menu to use with the entire class.

## *Suggested Forms*
- All-purpose rubric
- Proposal forms

Name:_____

# Reference Materials

| | | |
|---|---|---|
| ☐ *Dictionary Skills*<br><br>You can always find a word in the dictionary by flipping from page to page, but this is not the most efficient manner of finding words. Create a poster showing strategies and examples to quickly find words. | ☐ *Thesaurus Skills*<br><br>The thesaurus is a great resource for expressive language. Using the thesaurus, create a mobile with the words *great*, *wonderful*, and *big* as the top words. Under each provide at least five other words for each. | ☐ *Glossary Skills*<br><br>The glossaries of your textbooks have gotten together and formed a complaint committee. They are very unhappy that students do not use them. Create an advertisement for their campaign to encourage students to use them. |
| ☐ *Glossary Skills*<br><br>Create a scavenger hunt through one of your books using the glossary as your starting point and ending point. Have students find pages based on your clues. Have fun with its design! | ☐ **Free Choice**<br><br>(Fill out your proposal form before beginning the free choice!) | ☐ *Thesaurus Skills*<br><br>Write a letter to a friend telling about the exciting uses for words found in a thesaurus. Be sure and include a few new words in your letter as examples. |
| ☐ *Thesaurus Skills*<br><br>Choose a picture from a magazine you would like to describe. Using a thesaurus, write a descriptive paragraph for the picture using all new words as descriptors. | ☐ *Glossary Skills*<br><br>Create a brochure or pamphlet that shows the structure of a glossary, as well as the benefits to using one. | ☐ *Dictionary Skills*<br><br>Create a recipe card for the proper use of a dictionary to find words. Be creative! |

Check the boxes you plan to complete. They should form a tic-tac-toe across or down. All products are due by: _____.

# References

Anderson, L. (Ed.), Krathwohl, D. (Ed.), Airasian, P., Cruikshank, K., Mayer, R., Pintrich, P., et al. (2001). *A taxonomy for learning, teaching, and assessing: A revision of Bloom's taxonomy of educational objectives* (Complete ed.). New York: Longman.

Keen, D. (2001). *Talent in the new millennium: Report on year one of the programme.* Retrieved November 27, 2006, from http://www.dce.ac.nz/research/content_talent.htm

# Appendix: Book Lists

# Folk Tales

There are many books on folk tales available; the books listed are just a few recommended by the author.

Aliki. (1967). *Three gold pieces: A Greek folk tale.* New York: Pantheon Books.

Ambrus, V. (1992). *Never laugh at bears: A Transylvanian folk tale.* New York: Bedrick/Blackie.

Belpré, P. (1932). *Perez and Martina: A Puerto Rican folk tale.* New York: F. Warne.

Benitez, M. (1989). *How Spider tricked Snake.* Milwaukee, WI: Raintree.

Bogdanovic, T. (1972). *The fire bird: A Russian folk tale.* New York: Scroll.

Brown, M. (1947). *Stone soup: An old tale.* New York: Charles Scribner's Sons.

Cauley, L. (1988). *The pancake boy: An old Norwegian folk tale.* New York: Putnam.

Daise, R. (1997). *Little muddy waters: A Gullah folk tale.* Beaufort, SC: G.O.G. Enterprises.

Denman, C. (1988). *The little peacock's gift: A Chinese folk tale.* London: Blackie.

Duff, M. (1978). *Rum pum pum: A folk tale from India.* New York: Macmillan.

Hort, L. (1990). *The fool and the fish: A tale from Russia.* New York: Dial Books.

Hunt, A. (1989). *Tale of three trees: A traditional folk tale.* Elgin, IL: Lion Publishing.

Jensen, N. (2000). *How flamingos came to have red legs: A South American folktale.* Bothell, WA: Wright Group.

Loverseed, A. (1990). *Tikkatoo's journey: An Eskimo folk tale.* London: Blackie.

Park, J. (2002). *The tiger and the dried persimmon: A Korean folk tale.* Toronto: Douglas & McIntyre.

Scholey, A. (1989). *Baboushka: A traditional Russian folk tale.* Oxford, England: Lion.

Taylor, M. (1971). *The fisherman and the goblet: A Vietnamese folk tale.* San Carlos, CA: Golden Gate Junior Books.

Zemach, M. (1990). *It could always be worse: A Yiddish folk tale.* New York: Farrar, Straus and Giroux.

# Tall Tales

There are many books on tall tales available; the books listed are just a few recommended by the author.

Balcziak, B. (2003). *John Henry*. Minneapolis, MN: Compass Point Books.

Blair, W. (1944). *Tall tale America: A legendary history of our humorous heroes*. New York: Coward McCann.

Brimner, L. (2004). *Calamity Jane*. Minneapolis, MN: Compass Point Books.

Brimner, L. (2004). *Casey Jones*. Minneapolis, MN: Compass Point Books.

Brimner, L. (2004). *Davy Crockett*. Minneapolis, MN: Compass Point Books.

Gregg, A. (2000). *Paul Bunyan and the winter of the blue snow: A tall tale*. Spring Lake, MI: River Road.

Jensen, P. (1994). *Paul Bunyan and his blue ox*. Mahwah, NJ: Troll Associates.

Jensen, P. (1994). *John Henry and his mighty hammer*. Mahwah, NJ: Troll Associates.

Jensen, P. (1994). *Johnny Appleseed goes a'planting*. Mahwah, NJ: Troll Associates.

Johnson, P. (1999). *Old Dry Frye: A deliciously funny tall tale*. New York: Scholastic.

Kellogg, S. (1988). *Johnny Appleseed: A tall tale*. New York: Mulberry Books.

Kellogg, S. (1992). *Mike Fink: A tall tale*. New York: Mulberry Books.

Kellogg, S. (1993). *Paul Bunyan: A tall tale*. New York: Mulberry Books.

Kellogg, S. (1992). *Pecos Bill: A tall tale*. New York: Mulberry Books.

Kellogg, S. (1995). *Sally Ann Thunder Ann Whirlwind Crockett: A tall tale*. New York: Mulberry.

Lester, J. (1994). *John Henry*. New York: Dial.

# Alphabet Books

There are many alphabet books available; the books listed are just a few recommended by the author.

Cassie, B. (1995). *The butterfly alphabet book.* Watertown, MA: Charlesbridge.

Crane, C. (2001). *L is for lone star: A Texas alphabet.* Chelsea, MI: Sleeping Bear Press.

Dahl, M. (2004). *Alphabet soup: A book of riddles about letters.* Minneapolis, MN: Picture Window Books.

Edwards, P. (1999). *The wacky wedding: A book of alphabet antics.* New York: Hyperion Books for Children.

Fain, K. (1993). *Handsigns: A sign language alphabet.* San Francisco: Chronicle Books.

Feelings, M. (1974). *Jambo means hello: Swahili alphabet book.* New York: Dial.

Fisher, L. (1985). *Alphabet art: Thirteen ABCs from around the world.* New York: Four Winds Press.

Hoberman, M. (1974). *Nuts to you & nuts to me: An alphabet of poems.* New York: Knopf.

Johnson, S. (1999). *Alphabet city.* New York: Puffin.

Joyce, S. (1998). *Alphabet riddles.* Columbus, NC: Peel Productions.

MacDonald, R. (2003). *Achoo! bang! crash!: The noisy alphabet.* Brookfield, CT: Roaring Brook Press.

Pallotta, J. (1986). *The ocean alphabet book.* Watertown, MA: Charlesbridge.

Pallotta, J. (1989). *The yucky reptile alphabet book.* Watertown, MA: Charlesbridge.

Pallotta, J. (1990). *The jet alphabet book.* Watertown, MA: Charlesbridge.

Pallotta, J. (1991). *The dinosaur alphabet book.* Watertown, MA: Charlesbridge.

Pallotta, J. (1991). *The underwater alphabet book.* Watertown, MA: Charlesbridge.

Pallotta, J. (1994). *The spice alphabet book: Herbs, spices, and other natural flavors.* Watertown, MA: Charlesbridge.

Pallotta, J. (2002). *The skull alphabet book.* Watertown, MA: Charlesbridge.

Schnur, S. (1999). *Spring: An alphabet acrostic.* New York: Clarion Books.

Schwartz, D. (1998). *G is for googol: A math alphabet book.* Berkeley, CA: Tricycle Press.

Tapahonso, L. (1995). *Navajo ABC: A Diné alphabet book.* New York: Macmillan Books for Young Readers.

Van Allsburg, C. (1987). *The alphabet theatre proudly presents The Z Was Zapped: A play in twenty-six acts.* Boston: Houghton Mifflin.

Wargin, K. (2004). *M is for melody: A music alphabet.* Chelsea, MI: Sleeping Bear Press.

Yorinks, A. (1999). *The alphabet atlas.* Delray Beach, FL: Winslow Press.

# About the Author

After living in the small town of Roscommon, MI, and attending Grand Valley State University, Laurie met a goal she set for herself during her freshman year of high school and began her teaching career by teaching science overseas for 5 years in American schools in both Mexico and Brazil. After returning to the U.S., she taught middle school advanced-level science for 9 years in Houston, TX, before taking a position in the school district's gifted office as a master teacher. This is where she found her true calling—working with the teachers of gifted students; presenting practical, hands-on staff development; and helping teachers develop lessons that better meet the academic needs of gifted children. Currently, she is a full-time independent gifted and science education consultant, traveling throughout the state of Texas and providing staff development for teachers of the gifted and administrators, as well as helping school districts meet their science needs.